Grandma's Hands
The Heart and Soul of
New Orleans Cooking

Grandma's Hands
The Heart and Soul of
New Orleans Cooking

Deirdre T. Guion

CAP PUBLISHING & LITERARY CO.

Edited by: Avaneda D. Hobbs, Ed.D.
Cover and artwork by Pat Kabore

ISBN: 1-878898-17-5
LCCN: 98-070690

99 98 97 96 95   10 9 8 7 6
Printed in the United States of America

CAP BOOKS
P.O. Box 531403
Forestville, MD 20753

Acknowledgments

In Honor & Memory of My Granny . . .
Blanche (Sue) Picou Ridge
The love she shared transcends mere mortal bonds.

First and foremost, I give praise and honor to the Creator, my Lord and Savior Jesus Christ for His mercy, grace, love and infinite blessings.

There were so many people who were an integral part of bringing this idea to life. Among those who I must thank personally and continuously for their contributions toward this book are as is usually the case, my family, close friends and people who have touched and inspired me throughout most of my endeavors. My heart felt thanks go to . . .

Sherry Crouse, who suggested that my Grandmother and I write a cookbook.

Antie Fran (Francesca Ridge-Robinson), for the endless phone calls, recipe quotations, laughing and crying sessions.

Uncle Chef Bob (Robert Ridge), for lovingly agreeing to share his technical expertise and, for always encouraging his "Ebo Pride."

My sister *Christy Guion*, for coming through like a champ with typing, editing and loving support.

My *"Nanny" (Henrietta Celestin)*, who unlike most of my family, actually committed some of our recipes to writing.

Kent Guion, my brother, who instantly appreciated the magnitude of this undertaking.

Tamara Johns, a trusted and valued friend who was there during so many critical moments in my life. She has sampled, tested, and edited many of these recipes and gave honest and heart-felt advice.

Phyllis Lockett-Martin, who put my skills to the test in Minneapolis, Minnesota. This is a part of her belated wedding gift.

Bridget Chisholm, whose friendship never ceases to amaze me.

Carol Nixon, my oldest childhood friend, who helped me keep this project in perspective.

Anica Howard and Lisa Sheppard, who willingly and lovingly got involved in several aspects of this book.

D.D. Adams, Cherie Knight-Batey, Alisa Collins, Gerry Patton, June Stewart, Michelle Varner Smith and Kristen Williams, who all allowed me to be far less of a friend than I should have been during the past three years.

Paullette Everett, my business partner and friend, who graciously endured my absence of mind while completing this book.

David Banks, who has always supported and encouraged all of my endeavors.

Arthur Jackson, who paid me the ultimate complement as a cook.

Maria DiMare, who showed me how we all have many more similarities than differences.

Bernadette Henley, in Nashville, Tennessee, who after meeting me for one day, contributed enormously to the content and form of this book.

Pat Kabore, our artist extraordinaire, who so vividly captured my thoughts with her images.

Monica Morgan, who introduced me to Pat and made me stay true to my word.

Nancy Wilson, Patti LaBelle and Gladys Knight, for serenading me through endless hours of writing.

Iyanla Vanzant, who revealed to me the spiritual process that took place when I embarked upon this venture.

Nikki Giovanni, who sparked a fire in me by clearly articulating the need for our voices to be heard this century at a book reading in Minneapolis, Minnesota, in 1994.

Dr. Judy Gebre-Hiwet, at Spelman College, whose unending commitment to the written word touched my soul.

Dr. Maya Angelou, whose interpretation of Shakespeare's 29th Sonnet, touched my heart.

Christopher Reeve, whose courageous spirit has opened the nation's eyes to the trials of people who have sustained spinal cord injuries.

The good women of Holy Cross Catholic Church in Durham, North Carolina, a warm and wonderful extended family who helped my Mamma "raise me up right."

Dr. Avaneda Hobbs, who held my hand through the entire process and made it a pleasant one.

Finally, *my mother, Dreda Guion,* who acted as scribe, organizer, researcher and family archivist. I love and appreciate you as my mother and my best friend.

Thanks to all of you, for without each and every one of you this book would not have been possible. I salute the divinity in each of you.

Table Of Contents

Prologue - Keepers of Our Culture

This book started as a project for my grandmother and me in 1995. At the time, I was very concerned about my grandmother and wanted to find something meaningful for her to do that she would enjoy. Several years earlier, Granny sustained a terrible fall that resulted in permanent spinal cord injury. This previously vital and lively woman was suddenly paralyzed from the shoulders down. As the years progressed she often became despondent and stated more than once that "she didn't feel useful." Understanding how she could even think such a thing was difficult for me, because she clearly epitomized the word matriarch. I also knew how much she meant to everyone in my family. Likewise, I knew how much we depended on her love and support. Even if you cannot move, you can move people.

It was suggested to me that we engage on a project to preserve some of our family history and traditions. Immediately, recipes came to mind. You see, I grew up in a family that cooks. Most if not all of the recipes were handed down orally while we learned how to cook. While there were a few commitments to paper, most recipes were recited orally. I knew that this would be a tremendous undertaking since my grandma had surely forgotten more recipes than I'll ever know.

On her 70th birthday, we held a big birthday bash at her church's reception hall (St. Joan of Arc in New Orleans, Louisiana). The birthday bash was complete with some of Chef Uncle Bob's best recipes. I gave Granny a tape recorder and a box of cassettes to begin the process. I even suggested a few of my favorite recipes that I would like to have (and would not have to call her every time I needed them). Now understand. This was no small feat. Besides enjoying the oral tradition, the cooks in my family do not usually take too kindly to sharing recipes. Nevertheless, I finally got some agreement.

While we made some good progress on the recipes with the help of my mother (Granny's eldest child), the process revealed some incredible stories. Embedded within the recipes were delightful stories of my family's traditions. Very soon, I was just as interested in the stories and culture that brought the recipes to life as I was with the recipes themselves. It was sometime in December 1995 that I decided this stuff is so precious -- it is too good to keep to ourselves. Therefore, the birth of the cookbook.

In July of 1996, Granny passed on. I promised myself as I wrote her eulogy that her legacy would continue. So, what lies ahead of you started as a family project. It has evolved into a love letter -- a tangible expression of love and affection that is timeless.

I urge every person who reads this book to earnestly commit some of your families' history and tradition to pen and paper. As our elders move on, it is our responsibility to keep alive their experiences -- their triumphs, challenges,

Deirdre Guion and Blanche Picou Ridge, known as "Granny," Mardi Gras, 1996

love and compassion. As keepers of our culture, it is our responsibility to keep family traditions alive -- to keep alive the family.

Chapter 1
Knowing Your Roots

"Roots are deep and they are real.
It doesn't matter what or where your roots are.
What matters is how you view them and what you do with them."

Chapter 1 - Knowing Your Roots

It is funny how we define "normal" in regards to our own experiences. For most, normal is basically whatever it takes to get you through whatever you're going through. I never really thought that my family was normal like the "TV people normal." That is, happy and smiling with all of their problems miraculously resolved within a 30 minute time span every week . . . normal like the Brady Bunch, My Three Sons and the Partridge family. Oh lord, now that's a whole different trip. Two single parents who had six kids and a dog between them. I mean two men raising three boys and, a single mother with four kids in a band. Naw, I never thought we were normal like that. I had no idea, however, just how truly unique we were until I was much, much older. By then, I had given up the Brady Bunch for the likes of Good Times, The Jeffersons and the Nightly News.

What I did know and do know is that my New Orleans roots added just the right spice. It gave me an appetite and zest for life that is not just on me. It is in me. Roots are interesting things. They are necessary for anything to sustain life. Yet, very often it is the cause of much distress in life (the good ones and the bad ones -- roots I mean).

Stereotypes of New Orleans often showed rag wearing, fat, greasy women with a pecan colored skin. These women would be using "roots" at their pleasure to lure, cajole or otherwise reek havoc on unsuspecting but probably worthy victims. These are just that -- stereotypes. You could basically find that "sistah" anywhere in any small town south of the Mason Dixon Line. She could also have a whole bunch of relatives doing the same thing undercover north of the Mason

Dixon. Talkin' some more about stereotypes, what about those Cajun women with accents thicker than molasses, full hips, seductive smiles and mysterious ways. Well now, that's another thing.

I did not really believe in or have an appreciation for this "type of woman." That is, until Granny started telling us stories of women with names like Veroniqué and Berta. These women, according to Granny, used to wear their clothes on the wrong side and read tea leaves. Nan Burt, my great-great-aunt, attempted to practice roots. But, was more like Esmeralda, Samantha's nutty aunt on the T.V. show "Bewitched." My great-great-aunt could never get her spells to turn out right. Others, some of whom made cakes out of cayenne peppers, placed them under people's houses. This was so they would not have any peace at home. Suffice it to say, while I do not practice "roots" (unless it is an extreme circumstance), I do have a healthy respect for them -- the women and it -- the mind game. The roots I do know about are more like ground up sassafras -- commonly known as filé (pronounced feelay) that you add to your gumbo. Or, roots of ginger -- the stuff that makes those gingerbread men come to life.

I grew up on food with roots. I'm talkin' about red beans and rice, seasoned with "pickled tips" and bay leaves, gumbo, jamablaya, po-boy sandwiches, bread puddin', grits and grillades. Not bad being raised in the Piedmont of North Carolina, wouldn't you say. Well, that's what roots do. They follow you, no matter where you go or what you go on to do later in life. Roots can give you comfort and support. They can remind you of the good times with the sweet sentiment of an innocent child. And, roots can give you a soul felt appreciation of the times not so good. Times, that you've either lived to tell about, laugh about or choose to forget.

Roots are deep and they are real. It doesn't matter what or where your roots are. What matters is how you view them and what you do with them. Appreciating the best that life has to offer is difficult unless you have a real comparison to something other than the best. I would not know the difference between a baguette and a brown n' serve roll unless I had tried them both.

Most of the food I grew up with is now served as watered down versions in mainstream restaurants, cookbooks, and kitchens across America. I often warn people about eating these dishes out commercially, especially at chain restaurants. I really warn them to avoid anything labeled "Creole or Cajun" or swimming in red gravy (tomato sauce). I warn them because that poorly disguised excuse for New Orleans cuisine can ruin your palate and consequently your appreciation for the real thing. Now don't get me wrong. I have had several good Creole and Cajun dishes all across America. However, none of it was generated from the kitchen of a chain restaurant. Let me stop right now before I offend anyone who "got their recipe from a genuine Cajun right off the bayou" and say this. Cookin' and eatin' is just like livin', it's highly personal business. I'm not complainin'. I'm explainin'.

Cooking in Louisiana is very regionalized. There are about as many different varieties of gumbo as there are stoves to cook it on. See, recipes beg to be different, as different as the cook, the kitchen and the attitude that goes into preparing it. A word of warning: *never eat the food of any angry cook, it won't sit right on your stomach* (you may get a few of these warnings throughout the book).

The recipes in this book, just like the stories that go along with them, are handed down from four generations of New Orleans' back-of-town, chefs, grandmas, mamas, and aunts who take this business of cooking seriously. If nothing else, these recipes have stood the test of countless stomachs (foreign & domestic) and the test of time. "Bon appetite, y'all."

"Blue Monday"

It is called "Blue Monday" because people had to go back to work, after having had a pleasant weekend. Housewives washed and not having washers or dryers, decided that red beans and rice was the easiest meal to prepare. Neighborhood bars would have someone cook red beans n' rice to serve as lagniappe (a small treat), to their regular customers. This was to thank them for their business throughout the week. Even grocers would treat families to some seasonings for their red beans on Monday -- such as an onion or a bulb of garlic.

Red Beans & Rice

Yield: 8-10 servings

1 lb. Camellia red kidney beans	3 cloves of garlic, minced
10-12 cups of water	2 tbls. of parsley
1/2 lb. of seasoning meat*	1 tsp. cayenne or crushed red pepper
1 medium onion, chopped	1/2 medium bell pepper, chopped
2 large bay leaves	

Salt & pepper to taste or all purpose Creole seasoning (I like Tony Chachere's Creole seasoning).
*(Pickled meat -- tips or tails is what is commonly used in New Orleans but, hard to find anywhere else. I suggest smoked turkey, ham hocks or neck bones. A good smoked sausage can also be used to season beans.)

Directions:
Rinse and sort beans in cold water. In a large pot add water, beans, onion, garlic, green pepper and bay leaves. Cook over medium to low heat and let boil gently, stirring occasionally. Rinse meat with cold water and parboil in a separate pot filled with water. Boil meat until tender, remove from water (save the water) and add meat to beans. Add salt and pepper or all purpose seasoning. Stir beans occasionally and add water as needed. To obtain a creamy texture, add stock from the meat to the beans as water is needed. Be sure to skim the fat from the meat stock and taste the stock to make sure it's not too salty. Beans are done when they are tender, some skins are broken and, they have a smooth creamy consistency.

Steamed Rice

Yield: 3 cups

1 cup of long grained rice   2 cups of water
A dash of salt

Directions:

In a pot combine water, rice and salt. Cook over a medium flame. Let water
come to a boil uncovered. Once all of the water has cooked out of the pot and
rice is tender, cover the pot and turn off the heat. Allow the rice to steam for
5-10 minutes. Serve red beans over steamed rice. Yields 8-10 servings. Both
beans and rice freeze beautifully. To freeze rice, allow cooked rice to cool.
Place in a container with a lid or a zip lock bag and freeze. Storage time is
approximately six to eight months.

Jambalaya

Yield: 8-10 servings

6 cups of water   1/2 onion, chopped finely
1 tsp. salt   2 cloves of garlic, chopped
1/2 tsp. cayenne pepper   1/4 cup of vegetable oil
2 bay leaves   1 stem of celery, chopped
2 lbs. shrimp   1-1/2 cup uncooked rice
1/2 lb. cooked ham   1 large can of stewed tomatoes
1/2 lb. chicken cooked or canned   1/2 lb. smoked sausage
1/2 lb. crab meat or 1 large can

Directions:

Preheat oven to 350 degrees. In a large skillet combine oil, onions, garlic and
celery. Saute over a medium flame until clear or tender. Cut ham and sausage
into cubes. Add to the mixture of seasonings. Add all of the remaining
ingredients and cook over flame until shrimp are pink. Place the mixture in a

large pan and bake covered with foil at 350 degrees for 20 minutes. Remove foil and bake until rice is fluffy (not mushy) and most of the water has cooked out -- approximately 10 minutes.

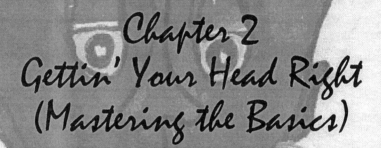

Chapter 2
Gettin' Your Head Right
(Mastering the Basics)

"Gettin' your head right is simple, but not always easy."

Chapter 2 - Gettin' Your Head Right (Mastering the Basics)

Before you even step into the kitchen, it is absolutely imperative that you "get your head right." Good food cannot be cooked unless you have got a good head. What I mean is that your attitude has to be right because it is reflected in the end product. No matter what you have been told in the past, nor how many pots have been scorched, or meals you've thrown out or tears you've shed over past culinary disasters, you will not become a good or even adequate cook until you get your head right.

Gettin' your head right is simple, but not always easy. First we must abandon all the "old negative junk" said about cooking. All that garbage about cooking being subservient and old-fashioned is just that, garbage. If you know like me, taking time to learn your way around the kitchen would be wise. Especially, since you could be eating anything containing God knows what and cooked by anybody these days. Here again, don't get me wrong. I just think that sometimes it's good to know where our food comes from, what goes in it and how it is prepared.

The second thing you must do is get a new definition and understanding of what cooking is. In a nut shell, cooking is creating. You take a variety of raw ingredients and spices, and combine them with a little chemistry to come up with a finished product. This finished product, of course, should be both edible and tasty.

The third thing is that you must believe that you can become a good or decent cook. Now this requires a little bit of an attitude. You know, the kind of attitude that you see in church every Sunday morning from a woman who knows her new dress fits just right. Or, the kind of attitude that is gracefully displayed in the strut of a woman who just left the hairdresser and knows she looks good. While it may take a little time, this attitude will come once you become comfortable and confident in your ability to whip up a good meal. Like my Grandpa used to say, "It's a pitiful dog that can't wag its own tail."

A Tail Waggin' Meal -- Shrimp Creole over Steamed Rice and Potato Salad

Shrimp Creole

Yield: 8-10 servings

2 lbs. medium shrimp (fresh or frozen)	1 16 oz. can whole tomatoes
1 large can tomato sauce	2 medium onions, chopped
1 medium bell pepper, chopped	3 cloves of garlic, minced
1/3 cup green onions (tops & bottoms)	1/4 cup parsley, chopped
2 tsp. rosemary	2 tsp. thyme
2 tsp. Creole seasoning	1/2 tsp. cayenne pepper
2 tsp. sugar	2 whole bay leaves
1/3 cup cooking oil	1/4 cup flour

Directions:
If using fresh shrimp, peel and de-vein. Rinse with cold water. Sprinkle a little Creole seasoning, place in a bowl and refrigerate. Rinse shells and heads in cold water. Place in a sauce pan covered with water. Bring to a boil and set aside. If using frozen shrimp that are already peeled, soak shrimp in water to thaw. Make a stock using chicken flavored bouillon cubes and set aside. Wash, clean and

finely chop onions, bell pepper, garlic and parsley. Place in a bowl and set aside.

Make a roux by combining cooking oil and flour in a large skillet. Cook over a low to medium flame. Stir continuously until roux becomes a dark reddish brown. Once desired color is reached, add chopped seasonings, tomatoes and tomato sauce into the roux. Continue to stir the mixture.

Strain shrimp stock and pour stock or bouillon into the roux. Add all remaining ingredients except shrimp. Cook over a medium heat until liquid has been reduced to one-half original amount. Place shrimp into sauce and cook until shrimp turns pink -- about 5-10 minutes -- do not overcook. Serve with steamed rice.

There is a difference between *Shrimp Stew* and *Shrimp Creole*. The difference is very simple. When this dish is prepared without tomatoes it is called Shrimp Stew. The sauce is brown. When tomatoes are added, it is called Shrimp Creole and the color is a reddish brown. Cooks Uptown prefer Shrimp Creole, while Downtown cooks favor the brown Shrimp Stew.

Shrimp Stew

Yield: 8-10 servings

2 lbs. medium shrimp (fresh or frozen)	2 medium onions, chopped
1 medium bell pepper, chopped	3 cloves of garlic, minced
1/3 cup green onions (tops & bottoms)	1/4 cup parsley, chopped
2 tsp. rosemary	2 tsp. thyme
2 tsp. Creole seasoning	2 whole bay leaves
1/2 tsp. cayenne pepper	1/3 cup cooking oil
1/4 cup flour	

Directions:
If using fresh shrimp, peel and de-vein. Rinse with cold water. Sprinkle a little

Creole seasoning, place in a bowl and refrigerate. Rinse shells and heads in cold water and, place in a sauce pan covered with water. Bring to a boil and set aside. If using frozen shrimp that are already peeled, soak shrimp in water to thaw. Make a stock using chicken flavored bouillon cubes and set aside.

Wash, clean and finely chop onions, bell pepper, garlic and parsley. Place in a bowl and set aside. Make a roux by combining cooking oil and flour in a large skillet. Cook over a low to medium flame and stir continuously until roux becomes a dark reddish brown. Once desired color is reached, add chopped seasonings into the roux. Continue to stir until all seasonings are well coated with roux.

Strain shrimp stock and pour stock or bouillon into the roux. Add bay leaves, salt, pepper and rosemary. Cook over a medium heat until liquid has been reduced to one-half original amount. Place shrimp into sauce and cook until shrimp turns pink -- 5-10 minutes -- do not overcook. Serve with steamed rice.

Potato Salad

3 to 4 medium potatoes	1/4 beli pepper chopped
1 stem of celery	3 medium eggs
1 sprig fresh parsley or 1 tsp. of dried parsley flakes	
1/2 tbls. yellow mustard	6 tbls. of mayonnaise
1/2 tbls. dill pickle relish	Salt and pepper to taste
Garnish -- paprika and parsley	or Creole seasoning

Directions:
Wash potatoes thoroughly making sure that skins are free of all dirt and debris. Place potatoes in a large pot with eggs and cover with water. Boil until a butter knife easily slides through a potato. While potatoes are boiling wash, clean, and chop bell pepper, celery and parsley. Place chopped ingredients in a large mixing

mixing bowl. Add mustard and relish to chopped ingredients. Remove pot from heat, remove eggs and potatoes from pot and let cool completely. Peel, wash and chop boiled eggs. Add to the mixture. Peel and cube potatoes and add to the mixture. Sprinkle mixture with two teaspoons of Creole seasoning or salt and pepper to taste. For best results, let mixture set in the refrigerator at least one hour. Just before serving, add mayonnaise to mixture to the desired consistency. A texture similar to a thick custard is usually good. Place in a serving bowl and garnish with paprika and parsley sprigs.

The Day Granny Got Her Head Right

Granny had the uncanny ability to tell a story. She came from a long line of story tellers who got together on Sundays to "out lie each other" and "out do each others' stories." New Orleans was known for its traditional "Monday White Sales." Ladies would dress up nicely with their white gloves and go downtown to Canal Street to get the picks of the day. This day was also known as "Wash Day." It was a perfect time to put on a pot of red beans while you completed the laundry.

If there were children in the family, they were usually adept enough to do laundry and watch the bean pot while the mothers would go to town. Granny's mother, Momma Nom (my great grandma) had a bad heart and could not do all of the work around the house. However, she was still able to cook. While getting ready to go downtown, she instructed the children to do their chores and watch her pot by stirring and keeping the fire low but steady. They understood and bid her on her way.

Granny was Blanche Picou. Better known as Sue, Granny had been watching and observing Momma Nom in the kitchen. She soon found herself lured to its mysteries. On this particular day, she decided to help her mother out even more.

Sue was ten years old and had been helping around the house for quite some time. She had never started a project by herself but this day, she decided to "get her head right." A hog had been recently killed for the family and her mother had boiled the head for hog's head cheese. The onions, parsley and the like had been chopped and were just waiting for her mother's return. Her mother had planned to work on the hog's head cheese after returning from town.

Well, Sue felt she could do this project and finish by the time Momma Nom came home. She went on to handle all the preparation steps. Mixing, blending and cookin' all the ingredients until it came to perfection. She had the cheese reduced to the consistency she knew her mother always achieved and realized one critical thing -- *SHE DID NOT KNOW HOW TO MAKE THE CHEESE GEL.* At this point she did not know what to do. A short time later, she heard a cousin coming up the walkway. The cousin was calling out so that Momma Nom would open the front door. Sue ran to the door realizing that help was on the way.

This was a cousin who could cook. The cousin looked at her and said, "Sue, your mama's sho nuff has this place smelling good. You can smell the aroma of that hog's head cheese at least three blocks down the street. Is it ready to eat yet? I know better, but, can I get some to go?" Sue answered sheepishly, "I am in BIG trouble. Mama didn't make that head cheese I did and I don't know how to make it gel." Her cousin looked at her and said, "Li'l gal, don't lie to me, where is your mama?" Sue said, "I'm not

Blanche Picou "Granny" and Brother Al

lying, my mama has gone to the White Sale and she had everything ready and I figured I would help her. I put it together just the way she would but I never knew what made the cheese gel." Her cousin cracked up with laughter.

Of course, Sue didn't think it was funny at all. After her cousin finished laughing, she told my Sue, "Bring me to the kitchen and let me see. Tell me everything you did and I will help you from there." According to Granny she brought her to the kitchen and told her everything. The cousin gave her the secret -- vinegar.

Grandma said her cousin helped her finish the cheese. When Momma Nom returned she could hardly believe that her Sue had finished the hog's head cheese. But, "Cousin" verified the whole story. That was when the kitchen became special for Granny. She now shared something very important and very special to her -- her mother's kitchen.

Kitchen Basics

Pots

In order to create a good meal you must start with good equipment. A good set of pots are an absolute must. Chef Bob recommends any Magnalite product. I prefer Caphalon. Both are very good products. Your set should contain:

Sauce pots	A roaster	A dutch oven
A colander	A strainer	A skillet

In addition to these, a set of pots for vegetables with tops that fit securely, is a good investment. Remember that you can find some great pots at swap meets or flea markets. You can also build your set of pots one at a time.

For Historical Purposes Only
Granny's Handwritten Recipe for Hog Head Cheese

Hog Head Cheese
Cover head + feet with
clean cold water.

Boil until meat is
tender enough to fall off
bones. Reserve water
Chop or grind meat

Cut up 3 large onions
1 sweet pepper
1 head of garlic
parsley, salt, pepper —
crushed red pepper

Place chopped meat +
seasonings into reserved
water. Cook until ½
the original amount.
pour in 1 cup of vinegar
Let cook about 10 min
more. Pour into molds
or pans. Chill + eat
"Bon appetite"

Knives
The next order of business is to get a good set of knives.

A chef's knife (which pivots when chopping)
A fillet knife   A paring knife (for cleaning and peeling vegetables)
A carving knife (for finished products or plain slicing)
A bread knife (for slicing baked products).

If you get all the above knives for $29.95 you will not be very successful in the kitchen because they will soon dull and come apart. Most of the best knives are in specialty stores or are sold separately at department stores.

Measuring Cups
You also need measuring cups in the following sizes.

One cup   One-half cup
One-fourth cup   One-third cup measure

Measuring Spoons
Measuring spoons are also needed. You will need the following sizes.

One tablespoon   One teaspoon
One-half teaspoon   One-fourth teaspoon
One-eighth teaspoon   One-half teaspoon

You will also need pot spoons for stirring. These are available as male (no holes) and female for straining (with holes).

Miscellaneous Utensils
Also a good riveted fork for frying (I call it a pitch fork), with a long handle, is necessary. A set of thongs for grasping, a heavy stainless steel wire whisk for

whipping and a stainless steel skimmer are also necessary. (The best knives and forks will have metal through the wooden end and be riveted through the handle.)

One set of stainless steel bowls for mixing are other essential tools that will be needed. The sizes should vary from one pint to a one gallon bowl. A set of Teflon baking pans is also very useful. Other important items you will need include a good set of oven mitts (those that are silver coated), pot holders, dish towels and spoon holders.

All kitchens should have a small and a large formica cutting board for chopping, slicing and resting ingredients. A can opener and knife sharpener round out the necessary items for your kitchen.

Be sure to look through your grandmother's kitchen for some of these utensils. Granny will usually have most of these and some others that she feels are essential. If you do not have a Granny whose kitchen you can raid, just check the kitchen of a good friend or others you know who cook on a regular basis. Remember, these are basic utensils and the store may try to sell you items you may not use. To avoid this, make a list before you go to the store and ask for assistance with these items only. If you do not get good help, go somewhere else.

Stocking the Kitchen

A well stocked kitchen is a sign of a cook ready for an adventure. There are some things I have found to be useful when already on hand so that cooking does not seem tedious and boring. Let's start with herbs.

All herbs are better fresh than dried, but, either if well preserved will give a satisfying flavor to meals. Knowing how to preserve these herbs is of utmost importance. When you are fortunate enough to find fresh herbs at your country market, neighborhood store, or a specialty store, don't be afraid to buy them in larger portions than needed for a specific recipe. There are ways to save these herbs that will keep them fresh and usable for another time.

One of the herbs that generally comes in larger quantities is basil. There are several types of fresh basil and they all are able to be processed in your kitchen food processor. They are also easily freezable in plastic zip lock bags for future use. If you are lucky enough to buy fresh herbs from a farm or farmer's market the same procedure applies to the following herbs.

Bay Leaves (leaves, ground) - Pungent taste with an aromatic flavor; we use in about everything including vegetables, soups, stews and gumbo.

Cilantro - Parsley like taste with a distinctly pungent taste; very popular in Mexican, Chinese and Italian dishes. Used to season and garnish -- use sparingly. It looks innocent but packs a big punch!

Dill (whole or dried) - Tangy taste and aroma; used in salads, sauces and with vegetables. Very good in seafood dishes.

Filé (ground) - Strong and bitter; excellent in seafood stews and soups.

Oregano (leaves, ground) - Strong, aromatic with slightly bitter undertone; great in Italian dishes, sauces, soups and vegetables.

Parsley (leaves, dried flakes) - Refreshing, but with a slightly peppery taste; it is often used in sauces, stews, soups, herb mixes, salads and garnishes.

Rosemary (leaves) - Sweet, fresh flavor; great in Italian dishes, seafood, salads, soups and vegetables.

Sage (leaves, ground, rubbed) - Slightly bitter taste; excellent in dressings, meats, sausages, soups and stuffing.

Thyme (leaves, ground) - Pungent taste with an aromatic flavor; excellent in chowders, stews, soups, tomato dishes and poultry dishes.

These are the basic herbs recommended for trial by the novice, and free use by the professional. Remember, each herb has its own distinct flavor and potency. Therefore, use them in restraint until you have tasted your dish. If more is needed you can always add, but you can't take away.

Basic spices for the kitchen are usually in dry form when purchased. Here are a few essentials.

Salt	Black pepper	White pepper
Garlic powder	Onion powder	Creole seasoning
Lemon pepper	Cayenne pepper	Crushed red pepper
Cinnamon	Paprika	Cloves
Ginger	Nutmeg	Chili powder

(Remember to use these carefully and to taste as added.)

Finally, the most important are the fresh seasonings available at your market. They lend themselves to being frozen or sometimes dried. Preferably they are fresh when you use them. These include onions, garlic, bell pepper, green onions, shallots, celery and chiles. (*A rule of thumb is that dried herbs will be measured in spoon measures and fresh herbs are measured in cup measures.*)

The Holy Trinity

As you will notice many of the recipes include onion, bell peppers and garlic.

These are affectionately known as "the holy trinity." If you start with the holy trinity it's hard to go wrong.

"First, You Make the Roux"

This phrase lets people know that you mean business. Called different things in different geographic regions -- roux (pronounced "roo") -- it is simply the mixture of flour and oil (or drippings). This mixture forms the foundation for gravies, stews, gumbo and the like. Chapter 7 shows three different ways to make a roux.

Chapter 3
Growin' Up In The Kitchen

"As a child, I was amazed when everyone who came to my grandmother's house ended up in the kitchen. The kitchen was nurturing and relaxing, and people felt comfortable in the kitchen."

Chapter 3 - Growin' Up In The Kitchen

The kitchen was and still probably is a focal point of family life in more than a few Black households. Since many Black families did not have a den or family room in their house, the kitchen was the gathering place. Also, the only telephone in the house was often in the kitchen. Naturally, the kitchen was an important place. Not only was cooking taking place in the kitchen but, bills were paid, homework done, decisions made and serious family business attended to. As a child, I was amazed when everyone who came to my grandmother's house ended up in the kitchen.

Now when people come to visit me, my mother, or my aunts and uncles, they generally end up in the kitchen. The kitchen was nurturing and relaxing and people felt comfortable in the kitchen. While I do not consider myself a formally trained cook by any means, I can "hold my own" in the kitchen because I grew up in the kitchen. Being an incredibly inquisitive child, I learned early that the best place to "be in the know" was in the kitchen. Not just to learn how to cook, but to learn about "grown folk's business." My ability and skill in the kitchen come in large part because of the patience of my mother and grandmother. They not only allowed me to hang out in the kitchen "with the grown folks" but, they patiently handed down their craft to me and the other children who hung out in the kitchen.

Granny raised seven children, worked as a domestic and managed an elementary school cafeteria for 15 years. She was and will always be the matriarch of our family. Her word reigned supreme in the family and in the kitchen. That rare combination of formal training, home training, creativity and compassion led me to believe that there was nothing on this earth that she could not cook and make it taste good. Not just good, but so good that you would need a towel to wipe the sweat off your forehead (a sure sign of good cooking in our house).

Granny took great pride in caring for her family and cooking was for her and is for me a tangible expression of affection. Believe me, cooking for people you do not care about is difficult. I distinctly remember that Granny did not discriminate in the kitchen. She was clearly a woman before her time who did not buy into that archaic notion that only women cooked. If you wanted to learn, male or female, she would teach you. If you did not, she would not force you.

Granny also had the uncanny ability, (probably because she knew us so well), to teach each person to cook a little differently, based on their personality and temperament. For example, it was not until we started writing this book

Granny in the kitchen

that it dawned on me or was revealed to me that Granny taught everybody how to cook gumbo just a little bit differently. Of course, the basics were the same. However, subtle differences are reflected in the different personalities and helped make that rite of passage special for each us. We never thought to compare notes since few of the recipes were committed to writing. More importantly, the end result was the same, "Good Food!"

Growing up in the kitchen taught me how to appreciate food and the preparation that goes into it. Once you have seen all it takes to get a live chicken from the backyard to fried on a plate, you can definitely appreciate the Holly Farms variety. That is, plucked, cut and wrapped at your local grocer. Growing up in the kitchen also taught me not to be afraid to try new things. The risks were a lot less as a child ruining recipes and having a guiding hand in perfecting them, than they would be as an adult preparing dinner for family and friends. Believe me, I experimented as a child.

I remember baking a cake one day when I was probably nine or 10 years' old. I added green food coloring and baking soda instead of baking powder into the batter. That thing tasted so bad that I could not even convince the family dog, (who would usually eat anything), let alone any human being to try it. I also remember my Uncle Bobby cooking fish sticks in tomato sauce for dinner one Friday night. Now that was a little tricky!

At age nine, I decided one summer that it was time for me to learn how to bake bread. The timing was good since Granny was taking a course on bread baking. She carefully walked me through the steps and explained the difference between rolls, biscuits, loaf breads and French breads. For a nosy nine years old, this was way better than any Easy Bake Oven. The chemistry also amazed me. Watching the dough rise under a towel was like magic. Baking bread taught me about hard work and patience. That stuff takes time and commitment! Since we did not have the luxury of a bread machine, we had to go it by hand and that meant work. Yet, the result was well worth it. To this day, I remember the smell of fresh baked bread emerging from the kitchen, and the big smile I was wearing on my face. Covered with flour from head to toe, I proudly announced, "the bread is ready y'all."

That particular summer, my mommy and daddy drove us, me, my brother and sister, to New Orleans. They went back to Durham, North Carolina, to get our new house together. When they returned to pick us up, they could not believe that DeeDee could bake bread. You would have thought I had won the Noble Peace Prize the way I strutted around the house grinning from ear to ear. Now just between me and you, to this day, I can bake bread better that most folk in my family -- with the exception, of course, of Uncle Bobby. But, that ranking is good enough for me.

Uncle Chef Bob, in his own words, said "Becoming a chef has always been a passion of mine." It started at an early age watching my mother with the greatest of care, and trying to duplicate whatever she prepared. This type of tenacity taught me to become a good cook. However, it did have its downside.

I can remember always trying to cook for my brothers, sisters, cousins and friends outside on a cinder block barbecue grill. It was made by my father for family barbecues. One day, when I was nine years old, I decided to cook out on my own. Cooking outside was easier because I wouldn't be seen or caught by the adults in the family. Also, the remnants of the evidence, once consumed could be easily destroyed in the canal across the street from the house.

The plan was that we would kill a chicken, a stolen one, and I would clean it, cut it up, season and fry it. I also thought we would enjoy having some vegetables to go along with the chicken. Finding the vegetables was the next hurdle to overcome. Clearly, I could not take them from my mother's kitchen because she would know that something was missing. In my finite wisdom I came up with an idea that I thought was the perfect plan. I would go around the neighborhood and collect canned foods to cook with the chicken.

I gathered my crew of brothers, sisters and cousins and informed them of the collection plan. Under the guise of collecting food for the needy, we would go door to door to gather what we needed for the meal. I was hoping to enlist their services to pull off the plan swiftly and efficiently. Of course, they were all too afraid to join in my scheme. They were, however, willing to eat the booty.

Being unable to convince any of them, I decided to go it alone. With a brown bag in hand, I went from house to house throughout the neighborhood telling these wonderful giving people that I was collecting food for the poor. The response was overwhelming. Since most of these people knew that my father had been recently laid off, they gave freely. I thought this was a wonderful plan until my parents found out. Though we were poor, my parents were proud and believed in making their own way. When they discovered that I had been begging, lying, and planning to cook and consume the spoils, I was in hot water.

My mother was appalled and my father was furious. At that time whippings were still very much in vogue. Believe me when I tell you that I received one from each parent. I was also ordered to return the cans to each respective neighbor, along with an explanation and apology for my actions. It was quite a painful experience for me. I haven't been much on collecting for any food oriented charities to this day.

I learned from that experience first to be honest and second to be responsible for my own food resources. Third, I learned never to trust brothers, sisters, and cousins when coming up with my cooking schemes. My sainted mother, being as forgiving as she was, decided that she would take me under her wings and started letting me cook with her. She carefully supervised my procurement of ingredients as well as how I prepared and served them. As I grew older and more adept at my craft, she became my source of encouragement and my greatest food critic. I owe most of my cooking success to her -- a woman of great recipes and cooking techniques. "

As you have seen, it seems we kind of had a coming of age around nine or 10, including Granny that got us all into this cooking thing. Here are a few of the recipes I was taught that adventurous summer and a few of Chef Bob's specialties.

Southern Butter Rolls

Yield: 25-30 rolls

2 packages of yeast (or 4 1/2 tsp)	1/2 cup of warm water (to activate the yeast)
5 cups of all purpose flour	1 tsp. of salt
1/4 cup of sugar	1/4 cup of shortening
1 cup of milk	

Directions:
Sprinkle yeast over warm water and let dissolve for 10-15 minutes. In a separate bowl mix dry ingredients and shortening. Add milk to the dry ingredients and mix well. Add yeast water to the center of the dry ingredients and begin kneading the dough. Turn out dough onto a floured surface and knead until dough is smooth and elastic about 10 minutes by hand or 1-2 minutes with a mixer. (You may need to add a little more milk about 1/8 cup to get the desired consistency).

Place dough in a greased bowl, turning dough over once so that the greased side is up. Cover with a towel, let rise in a warm place until doubled in size, about 30-45 minutes. *(Tip: to determine if dough has doubled in size, gently poke into the dough with two fingers. If the dough does not spring back, it has doubled in size.)*

On a floured surface, turn out dough and punch down. Pinch dough with thumb and index finger and form into 25-30 smooth small balls. Place on a greased cookie sheet. Cover with a towel and let rise in a warm place until doubled in size about 20-40 minutes. Preheat oven to 350 degrees.

Remove towel and bake at 350 degrees for 12-15 minutes or until golden brown. Remove rolls from oven and brush with butter or margarine twice. Allow rolls to cool on the pan for 15-20 minutes.

Whole Wheat Southern Butter Rolls

Yield: 25-30 rolls

Directions:
Substitute 2-1/2 cups of all purpose flour with whole wheat flour. Follow the instructions above. If you wish to use only whole wheat flour you will need to use 1-1/2 the amount of yeast and warm water shown in the original recipe.

French Bread

Yield: 2 loaves

1/4 cup + 1 tsp. of yeast	1-1/2 quarts + 1/4 cup of warm water
1/4 cup + 1 tbls. vegetable oil	1/2 cup less 1 tbls. sugar
1 3/4 tbls. of salt	5-1/2 lbs. + 2 oz. of flour
2 egg whites + 2 tbls. of water	

Directions:
Add yeast to lukewarm water and let sit for 10-15 minutes. Add sugar, salt and oil to yeast mix. Slowly add flour. Dough should be soft not sticky. Knead

dough on a floured surface for 8-10 minutes. Make a smooth ball and place in a greased bowl. Cover bowl with a towel and let rise until doubled in volume -- about 30-45 minutes.

Remove dough from bowl and place on a floured cutting board. Punch dough down and cut into 2 equal portions. Cover and let rest on table top for 10 minutes. Roll each portion into a rectangle. Roll dough like a jelly roll and seal the seam. Place sealed side down in a greased pan. Let rise for one hour and 15 minutes. Preheat over to 400 degrees. Mix egg whites and water and beat slightly. Cut slits into the loaves with scissors or a sharp knife, approximately every two inches. Brush egg mixture over the loaves. Bake for 25 minutes. Remove from oven and cool on a wire rack.

Presidential Cheese Cake

(This is one of Chef Bob's recipes that was given to him by a former chef at the White House. The President in office at the time liked cheese cake but did not like the graham cracker crust. This is a wonderful crustless cheese cake.)

3 lbs. of cream cheese	8 medium eggs
3/4 lbs. of powdered sugar	5-1/4 oz. sour cream
Lemon juice (to taste)	*(See appendix for measurements and conversions)*

Directions:
Preheat oven to 350 degrees. In a large bowl cream all ingredients together until smooth. Pour batter in a glass (Pyrex) or casserole dish. Place dish inside a pan of water. Bake at 350 degrees until done or golden brown on top. You will know the cheese cake is done when a knife placed in the center comes out clean. If knife comes out with batter on it, it's not ready. Once cool, slice and enjoy plain or garnished with strawberries or cherries. Store in the refrigerator.

Chapter 4
Taking the Show on the Road

"I've witnessed many folk scoff down the very foods at which they previously turned up their noses. You never know what you might eat or might even enjoy until it is prepared the right way. A funny thing is, the same is true in life. You never know!"

Chapter 4 - Taking the Show on the Road

Mama says I was three months old when I made my first road trip to New Orleans. While I do not remember that trip, I do remember several others. They were all special. We would normally leave "fo day" in the morning heading south. Often, when we were very young, Mama and Daddy would load us up in the car with our pajamas on, pillows, blankets and a variety of toys to entertain us on the long journey. Then, there was the traveling food.

I do not know who selected the menu or exactly how it happened that families, traveling by car all over the country, would have some of the same things. Nevertheless, that's the way it was. Staples in the traveling box were *fried chicken wrapped in a paper towel and covered in aluminum foil, boiled eggs, ham sandwiches, pound cake, pickles, chips and sodas (frozen the night before and wrapped in foil).*

As we tooled down 85 South, we would stop at selected sites to change clothes, use the rest room and fill the tank. Of course with a 1972 Electra 225, (a deuce and a quarter as it was called by my daddy and his crowd), you had 10-15 minutes to get it together. We did not waste any time.

I later learned that to tarry too long at these stops was not wise for Black families. Nor was it advisable to stop and attempt to get a meal in a restaurant en route. This did not phase me, my brother or sister one bit. We thought that eating in the car and listening to LTD or the Isley Brothers on the eight track was big fun. We would talk up a storm and play all kinds of road games. Sometimes we would have a picnic lunch at a rest stop. Here again, we really did not tarry too long.

Once we hit I-10 things got really exciting. My mama's eyes would light up and we could smell the salt water in the air. The car seemed to go on auto pilot as we made our way through Mississippi and into Louisiana. Crossing the Ponchatrain Bridge into the Crescent City was an absolute thrill. After riding for what seemed like an eternity, the end was close in sight. The heat and humidity hit us quickly as we opted to cut off the air conditioning, roll down the windows and catch a whiff of the New Orleans air.

When we were around the corner from Granny's house we would start blowing the horn to let everyone know we were within an earshot. By the time we pulled up, we had a small crowd of family and friends anxiously awaiting our arrival. They were all grateful that we had arrived safely. The ritual was the same . . . hugs and kisses for everyone, followed by my uncles raiding the leftovers from the travel box (especially the fried chicken). There is something about fried chicken wrapped in foil for several hours that is incredible. Granny ushered everyone into the house so that she could "get a good look at us." She went on to serve a good hot meal that would stick to our bones and help us get over the road weariness. That first meal was either red beans and rice or fried fish, shrimp and oysters with potato salad, French bread and all the trimmings. With my mama's six brothers and sisters, Granny, grandpa, us three kids and daddy, we had quite a gathering.

Over the years, several of our close family friends have traveled with us to share in our traditions. Reggie, the son of Aunt Lee, (one of mama's close friends) ventured to New Orleans with us one summer. He was about 14 years old at the time and nearly ate himself silly during the visit. He was so taken by the food that he decided to go home and make some gumbo himself. His concoction included bologna and hot dogs. I'm sure his dog wouldn't eat that either.

It was not until I was grown that my closest childhood friend ventured with us to New Orleans. The occasion was my Antie Fran's wedding, and Carol was finally making the trip. Carol had been exposed to our cooking through my mama since we were about eight years old. This time, she could finally eat the food in its place of origin. Of course, I'm now used to people telling me what they don't eat or don't care for. I've witnessed many folk scoff down the very things at which they previously turned up their noses. Now Carol had told me more than once that she did not eat oysters and was not a big fan of pasta dishes. Well, when ol' girl rolled into the "Big Easy," to help complete the wedding plans, she ate two whole Po Boy sandwiches complete with fried oysters. During the rehearsal dinner, Carol couldn't stop lappin' up Uncle Bobby's lasagna. While we hurriedly visited one of the tourist sites, The French Market, I thought she would "o.d." on coffee and beignets.

The lesson is -- *you never know what you might eat or might even enjoy until it is prepared the right way. A funny thing is, the same is true in life. You never know!*

Fried Chicken

2 fresh fryers, cut into pieces	Creole seasoning (to sprinkle on chicken)
1 tbls. garlic powder	2 cups all purpose flour
1/2 cup Italian seasoned bread crumbs	2 tbls. Creole seasoning (to put in flour)
2 tsp. paprika	cooking oil

Directions:
The Day Before
Remove all visible fat, and if desired, remove the skin from the chicken. Wash the chicken thoroughly. Drain off excess water. Place chicken pieces in a single layered pan. Sprinkle Creole seasoning over chicken (make sure each piece is covered thoroughly). Cover the pan with aluminum foil or saran wrap, and place in the refrigerator.

On Serving Day
In a large brown paper bag, place garlic powder, flour, bread crumbs, Creole seasoning and paprika. Fold the bag and shake until ingredients are mixed. In a

large cast iron pot or a dutch oven, fill halfway with cooking oil, and heat on medium-high. Place four to six pieces of chicken at a time in the brown bag, and shake to coat. Remove chicken from bag, shaking off excess coating, and place in pot skin side down. Cover the pot and cook on each side for 10 minutes or until done. Remove and drain on paper towels. Repeat until all pieces are fried. To keep warm, place chicken in a 150 degrees oven until serving time.

Linda's Little Old Lady Pound Cake

1/2 lb. butter (2 sticks)	1/2 cup shortening
3 cups of sugar	5 eggs
3 cups of flour (sifted 3 times)	1 cup milk
1/2 tsp baking powder	1 tsp vanilla

Directions:
Do not preheat oven. Cream butter, shortening and sugar. Add eggs one at a time, mixing after each egg. Sprinkle baking powder in flour after flour is sifted three times. Alternate adding flour and milk mixing after each is added. Stir in vanilla. Pour batter into a greased bundt pan. Place pan in oven and set temperature to 325 degrees. Bake 1-1/2 hours or until golden brown one top.

Uncle B's Lasagna

Yield: 6-8 servings

1/2 lb. ground beef, 1/2 lb ground pork	2-12 oz. cartons ricotta cheese
4 cloves garlic minced	4 tbls. parsley flakes
2 tsp. basil	3 tsp. oregano
1/2 tsp. rosemary	2 tbls. pepper
1 tsp. Creole seasoning	1 large onion, chopped
1/2 med. bell pepper chopped	1/2 cup chopped mushrooms
1 can tomato paste	1 large can tomato sauce

1/2 cup parmesan cheese
1 large box lasagna noodles

2 lb. mozzarella cheese shredded
salt & pepper to taste

Directions:
Preheat oven to 350 degrees. In a large skillet brown meat slowly. Drain grease and add minced garlic, chopped onions, bell pepper and mushrooms. Cook until all vegetables are soft. Add parsley flakes, salt, pepper, basil, oregano, sugar and Creole seasonings. Mix well. Add tomato paste, 3 cans of water, tomato sauce and 1/2 can of water. Cook over medium heat for 15-20 minutes. Add salt and pepper to taste.

Place 1/2 uncooked noodles in a large baking dish; layer 1/2 meat mixture, 1/2 mozzarella cheese and one carton cottage cheese. Repeat process with remainder of ingredients. Sprinkle top with parmesan cheese. Cover dish with foil and bake at 350 degrees for 20-30 minutes. Noodles will cook perfectly from the heat and steam of the mixture. Remove foil and cook for 5-10 minutes.

La Beignets

2 cups flour
1 egg
1 tablespoon baking powder
Cooking oil for frying

1 cup milk
1 tablespoon sugar
A pinch of baking soda

Directions:
Mix all dry ingredients in a bowl. Add milk and egg. Heat cooking oil in a skillet (about an inch deep). Drop dough using a teaspoon into the skillet once the oil is hot. Turn until golden brown on both sides. Drain on paper towel. Sprinkle with powdered sugar.

Of course, you can also opt for the packaged beignet mix, which cooks up beautifully. We like to use the Café Du Monde brand. Beignets are not complete without a good hot cup of Café Au Lait.

Café Au Lait

Yield: 4-6 oz. cups
4 level scoops of good strong coffee with chicory, ground
(Luzianne, Café Du Monde or RT are all good and should be available at your
local grocers).
1-1/2 cups milk   Sugar or sweetener to taste

Directions:
Brew coffee in 12 ounces of water. Heat milk until it steams. Pour equal
amounts (3 oz. each) of hot milk and hot coffee into a coffee cup. Sweeten to
taste.

Chapter 5
Nothin' Shows Lovin' Like Somethin' From the Oven

"You see, folks who grew up with mothers that were serious cooks, equate good food with the warmth and comfort that they felt in their youth -- a warmth and comfort that is a rare find for many as adults."

Chapter 5 - Nothin' Shows Lovin' Like Somethin' From the Oven

Through the years, I have heard this phrase quite a bit from my Granny and my mama. The older I get the more I believe it to be true. The ultimate compliment a cook can get from either a man or woman is "this tastes just like mama's." In a nut shell, that simple phrase says a lot. You see, folks who grew up with mothers that were serious cooks, equate good food with the warmth and comfort that they felt in their youth -- a warmth and comfort that is a rare find for many as adults.

There is an interesting connection between good cooking and fond memories of the past. Many people make a connection between good food with past events in their lives that were primarily enjoyable. I guess it is because many folks celebrate good times with good food. In my family, we celebrate life with good food. We have decided in our family that this relationship between food and the preparer never stops. No matter how grown the folks in our family become, there is always that little kid, wanting and needing a tangible expression of care and affection from a good cook. Based on this theory, we are about to give you some advice.

"Men and women both appreciate the efforts of a good cook." Men, please do not underestimate this statement. Women really, really appreciate and enjoy a meal

lovingly prepared by the man in their lives. More than once I have had family friends, ex-boyfriends and the like ask how we made specific recipes. Uncle Chef Bob has gained a loyal following among our family friends.

While traveling to New York on business, a few years back, I met an old family friend, Sergio. On this occasion, I met him at a night club in the city. Reminiscing over the past, Sergio continued to ask about all the cooks in my family. He even went as far as to confess that he had asked his mother and his wife to prepare some oyster dressing (just like the kind he had at my house one Thanksgiving). He admitted that neither of them could perfect the recipe. Sergio urged me to write out the recipe on a cocktail napkin right there in the night club. He "had to have the recipe."

My daddy had a couple of high school friends that would return to Durham every year for North Carolina Central University's homecoming. They would travel from Maryland, Washington, D.C. and New York, to gather with old friends and school mates. This was also an occasion for "big eatin'." Mama would prepare an incredible spread. One of the men, "Sleepy," (I don't even know his real name), would always say that "gumbo was sex food." Now, being a teenager, I dared not ask for an explanation, but I understood that this spicy soup obviously stirred some primal instinct in this man. Suffice it to say, good food touches the heart and warms the soul. Following, are a few recipes that "show lovin'."

Uncle Israel's Smothered Pork Chops

6 pork chops	1 large onion, chopped
1/2 bell pepper, chopped	4 cloves of garlic, minced
2 tsp. Creole seasoning	1 tbls. cooking oil
1-1/2 cups of water	1/2 cup steak sauce

Directions:
Wash chops and season with Creole seasoning. In a large skillet heat cooking oil over a medium flame and brown pork chops on both sides. Remove pork chops from skillet and set aside. Pour off oil in pan. Add finely chopped onions, bell peppers and garlic to skillet. Saute until wilted. Add chops, water and steak sauce to the sauted seasonings. Cook over medium heat. Let simmer until chops are tender. Serve over steamed rice.

Grillades (Grilled Meats)

A traditional early morning breakfast after prom night or Mardi Gras Ball is grits and grillades. This dish can be prepared ahead of time. It's simple, yet elegant.

Yield: 4-6 servings

1-1/2-2 lbs. beef round, 1/2 inch thick	1-1/2 tbls. flour
2 tbls. shortening	1 can tomatoes (20 ozs), optional
1 onion, sliced	1-1/2 tsp. salt
1/4 tsp. pepper	1 green pepper, chopped
1 tbls. chopped parsley	1 clove garlic, minced
1 cup hot water	

Directions:
Cut beef into strips. Dredge meat through flour, coating thoroughly. In a skillet, melt shortening. Brown meat in shortening. Remove and set aside. Brown flour in the same shortening. Add onion and cook until soft. Add remaining ingredients and meat. Simmer until tender. Serve with grits or rice.

Grits

Yield: 4-6 servings

1 cup uncooked grits   4 cups water

1 tsp. salt

Directions:

In saucepan, add water and salt. Let water come to a brisk boil. Add grits, stirring constantly until grits are dissolved. Lower heat and cover until done. If too thick, add water until desired consistency is achieved.

Fried Grits

Yield: 4-6 servings

1 cup uncooked grits   4 cups of water

1 tsp. salt   2 eggs, beaten

1 tbls. cooking oil

Directions:

Cook grits as previously described. Set aside to cool. Grease a 2 quart rectangular dish and pour cooled grits into the dish. Refrigerate for 2 hours or until firm. Cut into squares.

In a separate bowl, beat eggs. Dip squares, one at a time, into beaten eggs. Put oil in skillet and warm on medium heat. Place squares in skillet and fry for one minute on each side. Fried grits can be served with ham or bacon. Some prefer syrup on their fried grits for a sweet taste.

Potato Stew

"Makin Grocery" according to Granny . . . Most housewives in our neighborhood "made" groceries once a week on Thursday or Friday. By Thursday of some weeks, groceries were very low. Potato Stew was a good hearty dish to cook and serve because most of the ingredients were still available in the kitchen.

Yield: 4-6 servings

4 large red potatoes

1 medium bell pepper

2-1/2 cups water

1/4 cup vegetable oil

1/2 tsp. thyme

1 lb. smoked ham or pickled meat, diced

1/2 tsp. cayenne pepper or crushed red pepper

1 large onion

1 bay leaf

1/3 cup all purpose flour

2 cloves garlic, minced

1 tsp. parsley

1/2 tsp. black pepper

salt to taste

Directions:

Peel and cube potatoes. Place in a bowl of cold water. Put aside. Chop onion, bell pepper and parsley. Place chopped parsley in a separate container. In a heavy pot, place vegetable oil and flour on low to medium heat. Stir continuously until roux mixture becomes a reddish-brown color. Add onion, garlic and bell pepper. Cook for approximately 5 minutes or until seasonings come to a glaze.

Drain potatoes and add to roux mixture, stirring until all potatoes are coated. If using pickled meat, parboil until tender, and add to mixture. If using ham, add directly to the mixture. Add the bay leaf and water and cover. Cook until potatoes are fork-tender, not mushy. Sprinkle parsley on top. Serve with steamed rice and tossed green salad or beet salad.

Paneéd Meat

Pronounced "panade," is derived from the French word "pain" which means bread. Paneéd meat is a breaded meat. It is usually veal that is crispy on the outside, tender and juicy on the inside and, well seasoned through and through.

2 lbs. lean pork or veal - cut into steaks
8 oz. Italian or seasoned bread crumbs
1 pint milk
1/2 tsp. cayenne pepper
1 tsp. each salt & pepper

2 cups of olive oil
3 eggs
1 tsp. garlic powder
1 tsp. Creole seasoning

Directions:
Wash and season meat with 1/2 of the seasonings. Pour olive oil in a skillet and heat until very hot. In one bowl, add bread crumbs and the remainder of the seasoning. Place to the side.

In another bowl, combine eggs and milk and mix well. Dip meat in the milk mixture and remove. Place meat in bread crumbs and roll to completely cover meat. Dip meat in the milk mixture again and roll in bread crumbs one more time. Place breaded meat into skillet with hot oil. Fry on both sides until deep brown in color. Drain grease from meat. Serve hot with buttered noodles and steamed broccoli.

Oyster Dressing

1 loaf of french bread, cubed
1 large onion, chopped

4 stalks celery, chopped
2 tsp. minced garlic

1/3 cup fresh chopped parsley

1 tsp. sage

Creole seasoning

1- 8 oz. can oysters

Directions:

Preheat oven to 325 degrees. Pour vegetable oil into a large saucepan. Add chopped onions, green peppers, celery and garlic to oil. Saute on a medium heat until all vegetables are clear. Add parsley and slowly add French bread. Add salt and pepper and chopped oysters. If too thick, use some of the oyster water. Continue to mix until all ingredients are well blended and dressing is moist. Place dressing in a greased pan. Pat with butter and bake for 15-20 minutes until brown around the edges. Do not over bake as dressing will be too dry.

Chapter 6
Holiday Time

"Serving each other was and is an act of gratitude not servitude."

Chapter 6 - Holiday Time

Holidays were absolutely magical at Granny's house. I have never seen anything else like it. I'm sure my friends thought I was exaggerating when I relayed stories of goodies being baked and placed throughout the house. I now have corroboration from other relatives that this in fact was true.

While all holidays were special, Christmas was big time and the family went all out. The cooking had to start weeks in advance. By the time we would arrive in New Orleans around the 22nd or 23rd of December much of the work was

done. The house smelled of all kind of baked goods and because of limited space, they were placed on dressers and tables throughout the house. You name it. It was there. Pineapple upside down cake, coconut cake, brownies, Christmas cookies, chocolate chip cookies, crescents and pralines. The whole house felt and looked like a bakery.

THE CHRISTMAS MENU

Appetizers
Seafood Gumbo
Red Fish with Remoullade Sauce
Entrees
Roast Turkey
Baked Ham
Beef Roast or Venison
Side Dishes
Macaroni and Cheese
Greens
Mirliton with Shrimp
Green Bean Supreme
Corn Bread Dressing
Dirty Rice
Sweet Potatoes
Rolls
Punch For Any Occasion
And then of course your
choice of desserts

When we could stay until the New Year we had another major cooking holiday. Besides the traditional chitterlings, greens and black eyed peas, we would always have a party on New Years Eve. We would make heavy hors d'oeuvres and serve each other. Serving each other was and is an act of gratitude, not servitude. The hors d'oeuvres included hot crab meat dip, shrimp dip and, if lucky, either Oysters Rockefeller or oyster patties. Assorted  cocktail breads, crackers, egg nog and champagne to ring in the new year completed the menu. Here is a sampling of our holiday fare.

Laissez Les Bon Temps Rouler!
(Creole Phrase -- Let The Good Times Roll)

Appetizers --
Seafood Gumbo

2 lbs. of shrimp

1/2 lb. of ham

6 oz. oysters

2 lbs. chicken backs & wings

1 large onion, chopped

4-5 cloves of garlic, chopped

1 tsp. of parsley

1/4 cup of flour (for roux)

Water

Filé to taste

1 lb. anduille or smoked sausage

1 lb. of beef stew meat

1 lb. canned or fresh crab meat

1 lb. of chicken gizzards

1 large bell pepper, chopped

2 bay leaves

1 tsp. of thyme

1/4 cup shortening or cooking oil

Shrimp water - reduced

Creole seasoning to taste

Directions:

Peel shrimp. Wash in cold water and set aside. Wash hulls, shells, heads and tails in cold water. Place hulls in a pot covered with water and boil until reduced by one half. Remove from heat and set aside. Wash and chop onions, garlic and bell peppers. Set aside.

Cut stew meat and ham into cubes, removing any fat. Dice smoke sausage and rinse in cold water. Remove fat and skin from chicken backs and cut in half. Cut wings into three portions and discard tips. Set aside.

In a large stock pot place beef stew, ham, sausage, chicken backs and gizzards. Sprinkle with Creole seasoning, parsley, thyme and bay leaves and cook on low heat with the pot covered. As the meat begins to steep and juice comes from it, add onions, peppers and garlic. Stir and keep covered.

In a separate skillet add flour and oil and stir constantly over a medium heat. Continue to stir roux until it becomes a reddish brown. Be careful not to scorch (stirring will continuously help). If roux does become scorched, throw it out and start over. Once roux is reddish brown, remove from heat.

Add roux to meat mixture in the large pot once the seasonings are clear (most of the color is gone). Be careful as roux is very hot and may splatter when added to the meat. Fold the roux into the meat mixture and make sure the meat is well coated. Once coated, add strained shrimp stock and several cups of water to the meat mixture -- enough so that you can stir the mixture easily. Let the gumbo come to a boil over a medium flame and cook down for about 20-30 minutes. About half way through add chicken wing portions. (Do not add too soon as wings can make gumbo greasy). Add shrimp and crab meat and turn off heat when shrimp are pink. Add filé. Serve over steamed rice. Additional filé may be added at the table.

Red Fish & Remoullade Sauce

1 large red fish (5 lbs.)
   split, gutted and scales removed
cheese cloth
1 large onion, cut in quarters

1 pack of dry crab boil mix
2 tsp. of liquid crab boil
2 large fresh lemons

Sauce --
1 pint mayonnaise
1-1/2 tsp. hot sauce
2 bunches sliced green onions

1-1/2 cup ketchup
2 tsp. garlic powder

Garnish --
Romaine lettuce, cherry tomatoes and lemon wedges.

Directions:
Wash fish thoroughly but gently in cold water. Remove eyes from head and wrap fish tightly in cheese cloth. In a large pot add dry or liquid crab boil, juice from 1/2 lemon and onion quarters to 4-6 cups of water. Bring to a rolling boil. Place fish in the large pot head first. Make sure that the entire fish can lay flat in the pot. Poach fish with the pot covered for 10-15 minutes or until a large fork slides through entire fish. When done, remove fish from the pot (using large tongs and spatula) and place on a drain board to cool. In a separate bowl, combine mayonnaise, ketchup, hot sauce, garlic powder and sliced green onions. Mix well and refrigerate.

Cut cheese cloth from fish, open and let cool. When cool, pull back the skin and pick meat from the fish. Line a large platter with washed and dried lettuce leaves. Place on top of lettuce, working from the outside on the platter towards the center. Leave the center bare. Wrap the platter in plastic wrap and let chill for 2 hours. Once chilled, sprinkle the juice of 1/2 lemon on the fish, garnish the platter with cherry tomatoes and lemon slices. Place remoullade sauce in a small dish in the center of the platter. Serve with French bread.

Entrees --

Turkey In A Bag

Remove gizzards, liver and heart from turkey. Wash turkey thoroughly from the cavity to the outside. Remove any paper or plastic that may hold the legs together. Defrost turkey to room temperature. Add salt and pepper to the entire turkey front, back and cavity. Cut a medium onion into fourths and add to the cavity. Add one stalk of celery cut in half into the cavity. Add one teaspoon of cayenne pepper to the cavity. Make a mixture of three tablespoons of warm water with three tablespoons of paprika. Add one cup of vegetable oil, preferably peanut oil, to the mixture. Massage the mixture over the entire outside the turkey. Save the remainder of the mixture. Preheat the oven to 325 degrees.

Coat a brown paper bag with the remainder of the oil mixture outside and inside. Place the turkey breast side up in the bag and tie the end of the bag with string. Make sure there are no holes in the bag. Bake at 325 degrees for 10 minutes per pound. When done, remove turkey from the oven and let stand for 10 minutes. Remove string and cut the bag so that the steam escapes and the turkey stops cooking. Place turkey on a platter. Save the turkey drippings for gravy. Voila! The perfect turkey.

Perfect Turkey Gravy

Pour turkey drippings into a saucepan and place in the freezer for 20 minutes. Remove and skim fat and oil from top of a saucepan. Place a saucepan on medium heat and allow the gravy to boil. Reduce to 1/2 original amount. Pour gravy in ladle and serve.

Cornbread Dressing

2 bags of Pepperidge Farm Cornbread Dressing or
1 large pan of homemade cornbread   1 loaf of French bread
4 stems celery   1 large onion
1/2 bunch green onions   2 tsp. minced garlic

1 bunch of fresh parsley chopped
  or 1/3 cup of parley flakes
1/4 cup of vegetable oil or margarine
1 tsp. of sage
1 lb. of turkey necks, gizzards and livers (more gizzards than livers)

2 tsp. of salt
2 tsp of crushed red pepper
2 tsp. black pepper
1 lb. of chicken necks

Directions:
In a large pot, cover turkey necks, gizzards, livers and chicken necks with water. Add seasonings for boiling -- one onion cut into quarters, one stalk of celery cut in half and 1 teaspoon of red pepper. Let boil until tender. Remove from heat and let cool. Save the water. Remove skin from necks and discard. Pick meat from necks and chop along with gizzards and livers. Set aside.

Pour vegetable oil into a large saucepan. Add chopped onions, green peppers, celery and garlic to oil. Saute on a medium heat until all vegetables are clear. Add parsley and meats to the mixture. Mix all of the ingredients well. Slowly add crumbled corn bread and French bread. Add salt and pepper. If too thick use broth that was saved from the meat. Continue to mix until all ingredients are well blended and dressing is moist. Heat oven to 350 degrees. Place dressing in a greased pan and bake for 15-20 minutes until brown around the edges. Do not over bake as dressing will be too dry.

Screamin' Greens

2 large bunches of greens (collards, mustard and or turnips)
1 large onion, chopped
3 cloves garlic, minced
Creole seasoning to taste
2 tbls. vinegar
1/2 tsp crushed red pepper

1/2 bell pepper, chopped
1 lb. smoked meat
2 tbls. sugar
water as needed

Directions:

Wash, clean and chop greens. Place in a large pot and cover with water. Cook over medium heat. Add chopped onions, garlic and bell peppers to the greens. In a separate pot, cover smoked meat with water and cook until tender (save the water). Add meat and cook greens in a covered pot until tender. Once tender, add sugar, vinegar, red pepper and Creole seasoning. Stir well and reduce heat to low. Cook with the top off, until most of the water cooks off the greens.

Dirty Rice

Yield: 8 servings

8 oz. chicken livers	8 oz. chicken gizzards
2 large onions	1/2 cup celery
6 tbls. butter	1/2 cup parsley
1/4 cup green onions	1/2 cup bell pepper
2 cups uncooked rice	salt, pepper & cayenne to taste
2 cloves of garlic (minced)	

Directions:

Boil giblets in seasoned water -- one onion quarter, one stem of celery cut in half, and 1/2 teaspoon of cayenne pepper. Cook over medium heat until tender. Reserve water. Remove giblets and chop. Chop onion, parsley, green onions, celery, bell pepper and garlic.

In a large pot melt butter and saute chopped vegetables. Saute until tender. Add chopped giblets, salt, pepper and cayenne pepper to saute mixture. Stir in uncooked rice mix until all rice is coated. Add reserved water and stir frequently to avoid sticking. Cook and stir for 5-10 minutes. Add salt, pepper and cayenne pepper to taste. Transfer mixture into a large greased baking pan or casserole dish and pat with butter. Cover and bake at 350 degrees for 20 minutes or until rice is tender. If needed, additional water may be added. Uncover and bake for 5-10 minutes.

Desserts --

Pineapple Upside Down Cake

Topping --

1 stick of butter (1/2 cup)	1 cup brown sugar
1 can pineapple slices	small jar Maraschino cherries

Cake --

1 stick butter (1/2 cup)	1 cup of milk
1 cup sugar	3 cups flour
2 eggs	4 tsp. baking powder
1 tsp. salt	

Directions:

Topping --

In a saucepan, melt butter and sugar. Cook until sugar is completely dissolved and mixture begins to bubble. Pour mixture into a 9 x 13 greased pan. Place pineapple rings into the pan and add cherries in the center of the pineapple rings.

Cake --

Cream butter and sugar in a large mixing bowl. Add eggs to the mixture one at a time. Mix between each egg. In a separate bowl, sift flour, baking powder and salt. Alternately add a little milk and flour to the mixture. Pour cake batter into the pan with topping mixture. Bake at 350 degrees until golden brown. Remove pan from oven, turn out onto a plate and let cool (topping will set as cake cools.)

Sugar Cookies

Yield: 24 cookies

3/4 cup butter or margarine
2 eggs, beaten
1-5/8 tsp. baking powder
1/2 tbls. vanilla extract

1 cup sugar
2-1/8 cup sifted all purpose flour
1/2 tsp. salt

Directions:
Preheat oven to 350 degrees. Cream butter or margarine and sugar together.
Add beaten eggs until well blended. Sift flour, salt, and baking powder together.
Add vanilla and flour to creamed mixture. Stir gently until well blended. Grease
a cookie sheet. Drop cookie dough onto the greased cookie sheet with a teaspoon.
Place in oven for 10-12 minutes or until cookies become brown around the edges.
Remove from the oven immediately and place cookies on cake rack to cool.

Chocolate Chip Cookies

2-1/2 cups all purpose flour
1/4 tsp. salt
1/2 cup white sugar
2 large eggs
2 cups chocolate chips

1/2 tsp. baking soda
1 cup dark brown sugar
1 cup butter or margarine, softened
2 tsp. vanilla extract

Directions:
Preheat oven to 350 degrees. Cream butter or margarine and sugars together.
Add eggs to the creamed mixture. Gradually, add all other ingredients until well
blended. Drop cookies on a greased cookie sheet with a teaspoon. Place in oven
for 10-12 minutes or until golden brown. Remove cookies from sheet. Place on a
cake rack to cool.

Crescent Cookies

Yield: 40-42 cookies

1/2 cup unsalted butter	6 tbls. powdered sugar
1-1/4 cup all purpose flour	1 cup ground walnuts
1 tsp. vanilla extract	garnish - powdered sugar

Directions:

Preheat oven to 325 degrees. In a mixing bowl, cream butter and sugar. Mix in remaining ingredients to make a smooth dough. Roll dough to approximately 1/4 inch thick. Cut out with a crescent shaped cutter. Reroll scraps and cut. Bake on ungreased cookie sheet for 10-30 minutes. Let cool. Dust with powdered sugar.

Christmas Ribbon Cookies

Yield: 75-100 cookies

2 eggs	3 sticks of butter
1-1/2 cups of sugar	6 cups of all purpose flour - (sifted once)
1 tsp. of vanilla	1-1/2 tsp. of red & green food coloring as needed

Directions:

Cream butter and sugar. Slowly add eggs and vanilla. Fold flour into the mixture and mix well. Divide dough into three parts. Keep one part white, add red food coloring to one part and green food coloring to the third part. Line a rectangular pan with waxed paper. Roll each portion of dough into the pan until it covers the wax paper. Start with the red dough and follow with the plain dough. Top with the green dough. Refrigerate over night. Preheat oven to 350 degrees. Turn dough out onto a floured board and remove wax paper. Cut dough into 1/4 inch vertical strips and then cut them into 1-1/2 lengths. Place on a greased cookie sheet. Bake 10-20 minutes or until edges are golden brown at 350 degrees.

Festive Occasions --

Mama and Daddy's 1963 wedding

Festive Punch For Any Occasion

Granny served this punch at my mother's 1963 wedding.

Yield: 50

5 quarts of cold water
3 cups of lemon juice
5 cups of orange juice

8 cups of sugar
9 cups of pineapple juice

Directions:
Boil water and sugar until sugar completely dissolves. Let cool then add all of the other ingredients. Serve chilled over ice. This punch can be garnished with lemon slices, orange slices or pineapple chunks.

Petits Fours

I remember watching my Mama and Uncle Chef Bob making petits fours for my cousin Janice's wedding. They cut them into diamonds and dipped them in icing that matched her wedding colors.

Cake --

2-1/4 cups all purpose flour
2/3 cup shortening
3-1/2 tsp. baking powder
1 teaspoon almond extract

1-2/3 cups sugar
1-1/4 cups milk
1 tsp. salt
5 egg whites

Icing --

8 cups powdered sugar
1/2 cup light corn syrup

1/2 cup water
2 tsp. almond extract

Directions:

Cake --

Heat oven to 350 degrees. Grease and flour pan. Mix dry ingredients together, flour, sugar, baking powder and salt. Add shortening, milk and almond extract. Mix well 2-3 minutes with a mixer. Beat in egg whites and mix for another two minutes. Pour into pan. Bake 25-30 minutes or until a toothpick inserted into the center comes out clean. Cool completely. Cut cake into small squares, rounds, diamonds or hearts.

Icing --

Mix all ingredients in a pan inside a pan of water or double boiler until smooth. Heat just until the mixture is lukewarm. Remove from heat. Let glaze remain over hot water to prevent thickening. If necessary, stir in hot water, a little at a time until icing is smooth again. Place cakes, one at a time, on a wire rack over a large bowl. Pour enough icing over top to cover the top and sides of each cake. (Icing can be warmed and used again if it gets too thick.)

New Year's Eve Fare --

Crab Meat Dip

1 lb. lump crab meat

1/4 cup green onions, chopped

1 8 oz. package cream cheese

2 tbls. sour cream

2 tsp. Worcestershire sauce

1/4 cup onion, chopped

2 tsp. garlic

1 tbls. butter

1 tsp. Creole seasoning

1 tsp. Tabasco sauce

Directions:

In a medium pot melt butter and add chopped garlic and onions. Cook over low

heat until vegetables are clear. Add cream cheese and sour cream to the mixture.
Stir occasionally until cream cheese is completely melted. Add Worcestershire,
Tabasco and Creole seasoning. Stir continuously to avoid sticking. Add crab
meat, lower heat and cook for 5-10 minutes. Serve hot on crackers or cocktail
bread.

Shrimp Dip

2 lbs. boiled shrimp	1 bunch green onions
1 8 oz. package cream cheese	2-4 tbls. mayonnaise
3 tbls. lemon juice	1 tbls. Worcestershire
1 tbls. hot sauce	salt & pepper to taste
garnish -- parsley flakes	

Directions:
Soften cream cheese with lemon juice. Add chopped green onions and shrimp to
cream cheese mixture. Add mayonnaise, one tablespoon at a time, enough to give
a consistency good for dipping. Add hot sauce and Worcestershire sauce. Add
salt and pepper to taste. Chill for 4-8 hours before serving. Garnish with parsley
flakes and serve.

Oysters Rockefeller

4 dozens oysters on the half shell	2 packages frozen spinach (drained and thawed)
1/4 cup butter	1/4 cup flour
1 oz. Herbisant	1 bunch green onions, finely chopped
3/4 cup bread crumbs	3/4 cup grated Parmesan cheese

Directions:

Thaw and drain spinach. Grind spinach with green onions. Set aside. Drain water from the oysters, remove any shell pieces and save water and whole shells. In a large skillet, make a white roux with butter and flour. Stir until mixture bubbles (10-15 minutes). Add spinach and green onions to the roux. Add oysters and Herbisant and chop over a low heat. Continue to chop until all ingredients are well mixed (about five minutes). Remove from heat. On a cookie sheet, place the oyster shells. Fill each shell with mixture and top with bread crumbs and parmesan cheese. Brown in oven at 375 degrees until brown on top and around the edges. Serve while warm.

Oysters Patties

8 oz. oyster and water

2 cups of water

1 medium onion

1/4 cup butter

Bouchee shells or bread rounds

2 chicken bouillon cubes

1 tsp. garlic powder

1/4 cup bell pepper

1/4 cup flour

Directions:

In a small sauce pan, dissolve bouillon cubes in water and bring to a boil. Set aside. Drain oysters, remove any shell pieces and reserve water. Puree onion and chop bell pepper. In a large skillet, make a white roux (see directions above). Once roux begins to bubble quickly, add oyster water and chicken stock. Stir until roux begins to thicken. Add oysters, onions and bell peppers. Chop oysters into small chunks.

On a greased cookie sheet, arrange Bouchee shells or bread rounds and place approximately one teaspoon of oyster mixture on each bread round. Bake at 350 degrees until brown on top. Serve immediately.

Egg Nog

1 12 oz. can evaporated milk	6 eggs (separated) save the whites
1 cup plus 1 tbls. sugar	2 cups milk (whole or skim)
2 tbls. vanilla extract	1 tsp. cinnamon
1/2 tsp. nutmeg	1/2 tsp. cream of tartar

Directions:

Egg Nog

In a large non-stick saucepan combine six egg yolks and sugar. Add evaporated milk. Cook over low heat stirring constantly until mixture begins to thicken (10-12 minutes). Add milk (whole or skimmed), vanilla, cinnamon, and nutmeg, stirring constantly until mixture is combined thoroughly, about five minutes. Remove from heat.

Meringue

Beat egg whites, cream of tartar, and tablespoon sugar together until soft peaks form. Fold egg white mixture into hot egg nog mixture. Serve immediately while hot. Garnish with cinnamon sticks or freshly grated nutmeg. If a little more "nog" is needed, add 1/2 shot of bourbon to each cup of egg nog.

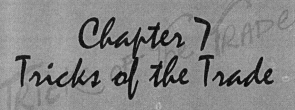

Chapter 7
Tricks of the Trade

"One of the best things about growing up around people who cook professionally, is learning some of their trade secrets."

Chapter 7 - Tricks of the Trade

One of the best things about growing up around people who cook profession-ally, is learning some of their trade secrets. Through the years, I have learned many tips from Granny and Uncle Bobby that save time and make cooking enjoyable. The following are several tips that I have been taught that I hope you find useful in your cooking adventures.

Different Ways To Cook Rice

Rice can be cooked several different ways and depending on the quantity needed. It may make sense to cook rice in the oven as opposed to cooking it on the stove top.

As a rule of thumb, you use one cup of rice to two cups of water. You can also estimate how much water is needed for stove top rice. Do this by filling the bottom of a pot with rice. Add enough water to reach the first joint of your index finger, when a finger is placed on top of the rice.

Stove Top Steamed Rice

Yield: 3 cups
1 cup of long grained rice   2 cups of water   A dash of salt

Directions:
In a pot combine water, rice and salt. Cook over a medium flame. Let water

come to a boil uncovered. Once all of the water has cooked out of the pot and rice is tender, cover the pot and turn off the heat. Allow the rice to steam for 5-10 minutes.

Rice In the Oven

This method of cooking is useful when preparing large quantities of rice. The same method, however, can be used for smaller quantities.

Yield: 6 cups
2 cups of long grained rice   4 cups of water
A dash of salt

Directions:
In a large pan combine rice, water and salt. Cover pan with aluminum foil and place in the oven at 350 degrees. Keep rice covered for 30-40 minutes until all of the water cooks out of the rice. Remove foil and let rice cook for an additional 5-10 minutes until fluffy.

Different Ways To Cook Roux

There are several different ways to make roux and it depends on the recipe. One way may be more preferable than another. For a wet roux, white or brown, Uncle Chef Bob suggests using slightly more oil than flour. You may see several recipes that call for an equal mixture of flour and oil. Uncle Chef Bob suggests, however, that a little more oil allows for easier stirring of the roux.

(Tip: Always stir roux with a metal or wooden spoon. Never use plastic as it will melt.)

Traditional Brown Roux

1/2 cup flour   1/3 cup cooking oil

Directions:
In a saucepan, add flour and oil and stir constantly over a medium heat.
Continue to stir roux until roux turns a reddish brown color.

Dry Roux

1/2 cup flour

Directions:
Heat a large skillet until it becomes very hot. Add flour, turn heat down to low
and stir continuously. Essentially, you are slowly browning the flour. When
the flour reaches the desired color (reddish brown), remove from the heat.

A dry roux can be stored for up to three months in the freezer. When needed,
remove from the freezer. Add stock to the roux before adding to the desired
recipe.

White Roux

1/2 cup flour   1/3 cup cooking oil

Directions:
In a saucepan, stainless steel or aluminum, add flour and oil, and stir constantly
over a medium heat. Continue to stir roux until it bubbles. The roux should be
ready after about 10-15 minutes. Basically, you want to cook the flour taste out
of the roux. A white roux is used for anything with a white sauce. *Never use
an iron skillet for a white roux. It will turn the roux brown.*

More Tricks Of The Trade

Boiling Potatoes
Always boil potatoes in their skins as they will keep the flavor and not get too watery. Notice that most of the recipes in this book that call for potatoes, unless they are specifically boiled, are boiled in the skins.

Boiling Eggs
A fool proof way to peel boiled eggs is to peel them under cold running water. By peeling this way, shells are easily removed. You will always get perfect whole boiled eggs.

Fresh Garnishes
Fresh garnishes are always crisper if you soak them in ice water before you garnish a dish.

Frying
Fry chicken and fish, skin side down first. This helps seal in the flavor and ensure even cooking.

Meat Stocks
Meat stocks can be refrigerated for one week or frozen up to four weeks. Each time stock is used, it should come to a rolling boil before it is added to a recipe.

Skimming Fat From Dishes
A simple way to skim or remove fat from any soup, stock or stew is to place it in the refrigerator until the fat rises to the top. Once the fat is at the top, skim with a skimmer or spoon to remove fat.

Cooking with Tomatoes
Whenever a recipe calls for tomatoes to be cooked, always add a little sugar to cut the acidity of the tomatoes. Another rule of thumb is to cook tomato sauces in an aluminum or stainless steel pot. Cooking tomato sauces in an iron pot will cause the sauce to turn dark.

Thousand Island Dressing

If you need to make a quick dressing, use a few tablespoons of mayonnaise, ketchup, and a little pickle relish, to make a quick thousand island dressing.

Custards and Puddings

When preparing custards and puddings that will be served chilled, pour custard into individual dishes. Spread a little butter across the top of each dish. This will stop the top of the custard from forming a thick film. Wooden spoons work well when cooking hot custards or candies.

Cooling Bread

Most breads cool best on a wire rack. The only exception are rolls. Rolls cool best in the pan in which they were baked.

Cooling Tips

Foods should be stored once they have cooled. Never let them cool for more than three hours before storing. After three hours, bacteria begins to form and could be harmful.

When preparing gumbo, one good way to help it cool and skim any remaining fat is by sitting the entire hot pot of gumbo into an ice bath. Get 3-4 bags of ice and place it in the sink. Sit the pot in the sink, with ice surrounding the pot. Stir the gumbo. As it is cooled by the ice, any remaining fat will rise to the top. The fat can be skimmed with a skimmer. Gumbo can be stored into separate containers and frozen or refrigerated for later use.

Kitchen hints

Place a pot holder or kitchen towel on top of a pot that sits on the stove. It may still be hot. The pot holder or towel lets others know that the pot is hot (once the stove is turned off).

To remove and absorb strong odors while cooking, place a small bowl of vinegar on the stove.

Chapter 8
Coming Into Your Own

"When you get to the point where you do not have to rely on recipes and often not on measuring cups, the point when it feels right, then you have come into your own."

Chapter 8 - Coming Into Your Own

If you grow up in the kitchen, there is a point in time when you come into your own. Families have all types of formal and informal rites of passage. In our family, it is making the gumbo!

During Christmas break of my junior year at Spelman College, I arrived at Granny's house announcing that this year I would cook the family gumbo. There I stood looking and acting grown -- with a "More" cigarette in my hand -- announcing to the family that I was coming into my own. In her usual style, Granny smiled, agreed and started getting things ready.

Making your first pot of gumbo is no small feat. Much preparation goes into creating this wonderful soup. Granny and I were alone in the kitchen. She carefully guided me through the process. Granny would give you the instructions, let you follow her directions and check periodically to make sure you were on course.

As Granny sat nearby, I distinctly remember her asking me to take the skillet of roux off the stove so that she could make sure it was the right color. "What is the right color I asked?" She replied "You know the color of a red black man." Till this day, that is the guide I use to get the roux the right color. She also asked me to remove the big pot of gumbo once everything had been added. She would then check to see if it looked right.

Of course, we are talking about a LARGE Magnolite pot filled with seafood, seasonings, roux and water. I had to call on the strength of all the gods to remove the hot pot from the stove so that she could see it. Once she examined it and tasted it, I was given the okay to lower the flame and let the gumbo cook down.

A few minutes later she announced "Deedee made the gumbo and it tastes good." My mama finally came into the kitchen. My uncle took a picture of me standing next to my first pot of gumbo. It was and still is a moment I treasure.

Everybody in our family comes into their own in the kitchen at some point in time. When you get to the point where you do not have to rely on recipes, and often not on measuring cups, the point when it feels right, you have come into your own. You have

Deirdre's first pot of gumbo

Christy's first pot of gumbo

seen it before like Justin Wilson on television who can exactly approximate the measures of things. He knows instinctively what a dash of this or sprinkle of that comes out to. While this takes time, it does happen. The following are a few recipes from folks in my family as they have come into their own.

Okra Gumbo

1 large bag of frozen okra
  or 1-1/2 lbs. of fresh okra
1/2 cup cooking oil (use with okra)
2 lbs. of shrimp
1/2 lb. of ham
water
2 lbs. chicken backs and wing portions
1 large onion, chopped
4 - 5 cloves of garlic, chopped
1 tsp. parsley
1/4 cup of flour (for roux)
Shrimp stock - reduced
Creole seasoning to taste

1 large can tomatoes
  (optional -- add 1 tsp. of sugar)
1 tbls. vinegar
1 lb. anduille or smoked sausage
1 lb. of beef stew meat
1 lb. canned or fresh crab meat
1 lb. of chicken gizzards
1 large bell pepper, chopped
2 bay leaves
1 tsp. of thyme
1/4 cup cooking oil (for roux)
2 tsp. filé
filé to taste at the table

Directions:

Wash and slice fresh okra. In a large skillet add okra and 1/2 cup of oil. Fry on low heat uncovered and stir occasionally. Add vinegar and continue to stir and cook until seeds are pink and gelatinous matter evaporates. Should take about 30-45 minutes. If adding tomatoes, add to fried okra, sprinkle with sugar and cook for five minutes. Remove from heat and set aside.

Peel shrimp. Wash and set aside. Wash hulls, shells, heads and tails in cold water. Place hulls in a pot covered with water. Boil until reduced by one half. Remove from heat and set aside.

Wash and chop onions, garlic and bell peppers. Set aside. Cut stew meat and ham into cubes, removing any fat. Dice smoke sausage and rinse in cold water. Remove fat and skin from chicken backs and cut in half. Cut wings into three portions. Discard the wing tips.

In a large stock pot place beef stew, ham, sausage, chicken backs and gizzards. Sprinkle with Creole seasoning, parsley, thyme and bay leaves and cook on low heat with the pot covered. As the meat begins to steep -- juice comes from it -- add onions, peppers and garlic. Stir and keep covered.

In a separate skillet, add flour and remaining oil. Stir constantly over a medium heat. Continue to stir roux until it becomes a reddish brown. Be careful not to scorch (stirring continuously will help). If roux does become scorched, throw it out and start over. Once roux is reddish brown, remove from heat.

Add roux to meat mixture in the large pot once the seasonings are clear. Add okra and tomatoes. Be careful as roux is very hot and may splatter when added to the meat. Fold the roux into the meat mixture and make sure the meat is well coated with the roux. Once coated, add strained shrimp stock and several cups of water to the meat mixture -- enough so that you can stir the mixture easily. Let the gumbo come to a boil over a medium flame and cook down for about 20-30 minutes. About halfway through cooking time (10-15 minutes) add wing portions. Add shrimp, crab meat and filé. Turn off heat when shrimp are pink. Serve over steamed rice. More filé may be added at the table.

Fran's Batter Fried Chicken and Marinated Salad

Battered Fried Chicken

2 fresh fryers, cut into pieces
1 cup Italian bread crumbs
1 tbls. garlic powder
2 tbls. Creole seasoning (to put in flour)
cooking oil

Creole seasoning (to sprinkle on chicken)
2 cups all purpose flour
2 tsp. paprika

Directions:

Batter *(This is kinda like making a pancake batter)*
3 eggs well beaten   1-1/2 cups milk

1 tsp. baking powder 1-1/2 cups flour
1 tsp. pepper 1 tsp. garlic powder
1 tsp. salt

Directions:
The Day Before
Remove all visible fat, and if desired, remove the skin. Wash chicken thoroughly. Drain off excess water. Place chicken pieces in a single layered pan. Sprinkle Creole seasoning over chicken (make sure each piece is covered thoroughly). Cover the pan with aluminum foil or saran wrap, and place in the refrigerator.

On Serving Day
In a large brown paper bag, place garlic powder, flour, bread crumbs, Creole seasoning and paprika. Set aside. Fold the bag and shake until ingredients are mixed. In a large bowl, mix eggs, flour, milk and baking powder. In a large cast iron pot or a dutch oven, fill three quarters of the way with cooking oil, and heat on medium.

Place four to six pieces of chicken at a time in the brown bag. Shake to coat. Remove chicken from bag, shaking off excess coating, and dip in the batter. Let excess batter drip off then place in the pot skin side down. Cover the pot and cook. Check frequently to make sure the outside coating does not turn brown too quickly. Chicken is done when it floats to the top of the oil. Remove and drain on paper towels. Repeat until all pieces are fried. To keep warm, place chicken in a 150 degree oven until serving time.

Marinated Salad

2 medium bell peppers 3 large tomatoes
8 oz. bottle Italian dressing 2 tsp. Creole seasoning
1 tsp. fresh dried basil

Directions:
Cut bell peppers in half. Core and remove seeds. Wash thoroughly. Remove stem, core and bottom of tomatoes. Wash thoroughly. Cut bell peppers in 1/8 inch strips. Cut tomatoes into wedges (approximately six pieces). Place bell peppers and tomatoes in a deep bowl with a lid. Sprinkle basil and Creole seasoning over the vegetables, toss until they are well coated. Pour 4-8 ounces of dressing over the vegetables. Cover and refrigerate at least two hours (overnight is best). When serving, lift vegetables out of the marinade and arrange on small platter, and garnish with curly parsley and cherry tomatoes. Pour marinade in a serving bowl to use as a dip or additional dressing for the vegetables.

Christy's Famous Meatballs

1 lb. ground beef	1/2 cup bread crumbs
1/2 tsp salt	1/2 tsp pepper
1/2 tsp garlic powder	1/4 cup onion, chopped
1 egg	1 tsp Worcestershire sauce
1 tsp parmesan cheese	1/2 tsp oregano
1/8 cup bell pepper, chopped	1 tbls. ketchup

Directions:
Preheat oven to 350 degrees. Mix all ingredients together and shape into small meatballs. Place on lightly greased baking pan. Bake for 20-25 minutes until brown and thoroughly cooked. Serve over steamed rice or with barbecue sauce as hors d'oeuvres.

Kent & Jeanine's Sweet 'N Hot Chicken
(Not for the faint at heart!!)

My brother Kent, has always enjoyed Italian food. We used to call him jokingly

"Chef Boyardee." I was hoping he would offer his manicotti recipe but, remember I told you my family can be a little funny about their recipes. While this isn't the manicotti, I think you will enjoy it just the same.

1 lb. boneless, skinless chicken breast
1 tbls. Creole seasoning
1 tbls. crushed red pepper
1 tbls. chopped onion
1/2 cup molasses
1/2 cup water

3 tbls. sesame oil
1/2 tsp. chili powder
1 tbls. Worcestershire sauce
1/2 tsp. ginger
1-1/2 cups sliced mushrooms
1 package frozen green peas

Directions:
Wash and cut chicken into one to two inch strips. Season with Creole seasoning. Heat a large skillet on medium high for 5-10 minutes. In one hand hold chicken, in the other hold sesame oil. Quickly add sesame oil then chicken. Stir continuously to coat the chicken with the oil. Add onions, ginger and chili powder. Stir ingredients well. Add mushrooms, Worcestershire sauce and continue to stir. Finally, add the hot stuff -- crushed red pepper followed by the sweet stuff -- molasses, water and peas. Stir and let simmer for 5-7 minutes until sauce thickens. Serve over rice or noodles.

Deedee's Lemon Meringue Pie

6 eggs (separated)
3 cans sweetened condensed milk
1 tsp. vanilla
2 tbls. sugar

6 fresh lemons
2 tsp. cream of tartar
1 tsp. grated lemon rind
2 Graham cracker pie shells

Directions:
In a large mixing bowl, add sweetened condensed milk, the juice of five lemons, lemon rind and vanilla. Separate eggs and fold yolks into the mixture one at a time. Pour the juice from one-half lemon into the empty pie shells.

Pour mixture into pie shells. In a separate bowl add egg whites, cream of tartar, sugar and remaining lemon juice (1/2 lemon) and beat until frothy. Continue to beat until eggs form a meringue with stiff peaks. Top the pies with meringue and form peaks with a fork. Bake at 325 degrees until peaks of meringue are golden brown. Cool before serving and refrigerate to store.

Antie Henny's Buttermilk Pie

1 stick butter   1 cup of buttermilk
1 tsp. vanilla   1 large pie crust
3 eggs   1-1/2 cups sugar
4 tbls. flour

Directions:
In a saucepan, melt butter and sugar over a low heat. Add buttermilk and vanilla to mixture and continue to stir. Beat eggs and pour into the buttermilk mixture. Add flour to the mixture to get desired consistency. Mixture should thicken until it reaches a custard consistency. Pour mixture into pie crust and bake at 350 degrees until the top is golden brown and filling is firm. Let cool before serving. Store in the refrigerator.

Antie Fran's "Plarine" Candy

For as long as I can remember, Antie Fran has been the queen of candy making in our family. She learned how to make candy from the nuns at the church. She learned well.

If you have ever had an occasion to travel to New Orleans and sample a *praline*, what you probably had was a piece of candy the size of a small pancake. The color was caramel with a white sugary tint. It probably tasted a little sugary and was loaded with pecans. What we make is commonly known as "pecan candy" or *plarines*. It is very smooth in texture and taste, is loaded with pecans and has a beautiful caramel color. According to Antie Fran, candy is made by trial and error. You use your senses to cook candy, to get just the right consistency. Be patient and give yourself a little time.

Yield: 2 dozen

2 cups sugar

2 tbls. margarine or butter

1-1/2 cups pecans or coconut

1 cup half & half cream

1 tsp. vanilla

Directions:

Combine sugar, cream and butter in a 3-quart sauce pan. Stir until dissolved and cook on medium heat until mixture passes a soft ball stage. (A soft ball stage occurs when a drop of the mixture is placed in a cold glass of water and beads like a ball.) The candy usually reaches this stage once it begins to caramelize. The candy should be boiling rapidly, almost blistering, boiling from the edge of the pot toward the center. Remove from heat, add vanilla and pecans. Return to heat and beat with a wooden spoon until candy coats the spoon. Quickly place spoonfuls of candy onto wax paper and let cool.

Mama's Lemon Squares

Yield: 32 pieces. Approximately 125 calories each.

1 cup butter or margarine at room temperature

1/2 cup plus 1 tbls. confectioner's sugar

2-1/3 cups unsifted flour

1/2 tsp. baking powder

4 eggs

1/3 cup lemon juice

1-3/4 cups granulated sugar

Directions:

Crust

Preheat oven to 350 degrees. Cream butter or margarine in a medium bowl with 1/2 cup confectioner's sugar. Add two cups of flour and stir until well combined with a wooden spoon. Pat evenly into a 13 x 9 inch baking pan. Bake for 20 minutes.

Filling

Combine eggs, granulated sugar, remaining 1/3 cup flour, lemon juice and baking powder in a blender. Cover and blend for five seconds. Scrape down sides of blender container and blend another five seconds. Pour over partially baked crust. Bake 25 minutes more or until golden brown. Cool completely on a wire rack. Sprinkle with remaining tablespoon confectioners' sugar. Cut into squares.

Uncle Tony's Barbecue

Uncle Tony has been the reigning barbecue king since grandpa passed away. While he uses grandpa's barbecue sauce, he has come into his own with grilling techniques. Here are a few of them.

Grandpa's Barbecue Sauce

1/2 can of tomato paste
1/4 cup sugar (or molasses or honey)
4 cloves of garlic minced
1 bottle Worcestershire sauce
crushed red pepper

2 large onions, chopped
2 tbls. liquid smoke
3 tbls. vinegar
Creole seasoning
1-1/2 quarts of water

Directions:
Place all ingredients in a large pot, and place on medium high to heat on stove top. Allow ingredients to boil until mixture reaches desired consistency (prepared barbecue sauce may be used to thicken consistency). Let cool down and put aside for later use.

Grilled Barbecue Chicken

2 fryers cut into pieces
2 tsp. lemon pepper
1 tsp. cayenne pepper

2 tsp. salt
1 tsp. garlic powder

Directions:
The night before serving, wash chicken parts thoroughly. Mix all dry ingredients. Coat chicken with dry mixture, place in a covered dish. Put in refrigerator overnight to marinade.

Prepare the grill by heating coals and hardwood briquets until completely white. Place large chicken parts on the grill skin side down. Turn chicken every five minutes until done. Repeat with other pieces. Apply sauce to chicken, coating it well. Place back on the grill for approximately two minutes to seal in flavor. Remove chicken from grill and serve.

Grilled Barbecue Ribs

Pork Ribs - Prepare pork ribs as instructed in the grilled chicken recipe.

Beef Ribs

Directions:
Marinate ribs with the dry mixture used for grilled barbecue chicken. Instead of marinating overnight, place ribs in a shallow pan. Cover with aluminum foil. Place in the oven on 150 degrees for approximately five hours. Remove from oven, and place on the grill until done. Apply barbecue sauce on ribs. Return to grill for approximately five minutes. Remove from grill and serve.

Grilled Red Fish

1 large red fish (3/4-1 inch thick)　　1/2 stick butter
1 tsp. garlic powder　　　　　　　　juice from 1/2 lemon

Directions:
Place butter, garlic powder, and lemon juice in a small saucepan. Melt mixture on a low to medium heat. Remove from heat. Brush butter mixture on the skin side of the fish and place on a heated grill. Brush flaky side of fish with butter mixture while on the grill. Cover grill. Cook for approximately 10 minutes or until meat turns white. Remove from grill and serve.

Chapter 9
Family Favorites

"Top picks from my family."

Chapter 9 - Family Favorites

The following are a few of my family's favorite recipes. We hope you enjoy them as much as we do.

Johnny's Barbecue Shrimp

2 lbs. large shrimp (shells and tails on)
1 large bottle chili sauce
1 stick butter
2 bay leaves

2 cups of white wine
6 tbls. Worcestershire sauce
4 tsp. thyme
2 tbls. sugar

Directions:
Wash shrimp in cold water. In a large skillet, melt 1/2 stick of butter. Add one bay leaf, half a bottle of chili sauce, three tablespoons of Worcestershire sauce and one cup of wine. Stir all ingredients together. Add one tablespoon of sugar and two teaspoons of thyme. Cook over medium heat until sauce bubbles lightly. Add one pound of shrimp to the mixture. Continuously turn shrimp in the mixture, until well coated and shrimp turns pink. In a large pan, pour shrimp and sauce. Place in an oven on warm and cover with foil. Repeat instructions above for the second pound of shrimp. Serve with warm French bread and a crisp tossed salad.

Smothered Chicken

Yield: 4-6 servings
1 fryer, cut-up

1 medium onion, chopped

1/2 bell pepper chopped
1 tsp. Creole seasoning
4 tbls. cooking oil
1 bay leaf
2 cups of water

2 cloves garlic, minced
1 tsp. each salt & pepper
1/4 cup flour
Creole seasoning to taste

Directions:

Wash chicken in cold water. Season chicken with dry seasonings and dust with flour. In a large pot add oil and heat over medium flame. Place chicken in oil and let brown on both sides. Remove chicken and set aside. Add chopped seasonings and any remaining flour to pot and saute until tender. Add chicken, water and bay leaf to mixture and cook over medium heat. Dish is done when chicken is tender with a nice gravy 30-45 minutes. Serve over rice, grits or noodles.

Stuffed Bell Peppers

Yield: 6 servings

3 large bell peppers
2 cups of bread, cubed
1/2 cup celery, chopped
1 lb. shrimp or 2 8 oz. cans
1 lb. ground beef
Garnish - butter and bread crumbs

1 medium onion, chopped
1/4 cup green onion, chopped
1 clove garlic, minced
1 tbls. parsley
salt, pepper, and cayenne to taste
1/4 cup of water

Directions:

Preheat oven to 350 degrees. Wash, core and cut peppers in half. Set aside. In a large bowl moisten bread with water. Brown ground beef in a skillet and drain. Add all other ingredients and mix thoroughly. Pour into heavy skillet or pot and cook for 5-8 minutes. Stuff each half pepper with mixture. Place in buttered deep casserole dish containing enough water to cover half the individual bell peppers. Sprinkle lightly with bread crumbs and place a pat of butter on top of each pepper. Bake until peppers are tender or tops are brown.

Banana Pudding

Yield: 6 servings

1 cup sugar
3/4 tsp. salt
3 eggs (separated)
3 large very ripe bananas

1/3 cup cornstarch
3 cups milk (evaporated or skim)
1-1/2 tsp. vanilla extract
24 vanilla wafers

Directions:

Preheat oven to 350 degrees. In a saucepan mix 2/3 cup of sugar, cornstarch and salt. Gradually add milk. Cook over low heat stirring constantly until mixture thickens. In a small bowl add egg yolks. Slowly add small amounts of some hot sugar mixture to egg yolks, stirring constantly. Pour egg yolk mixture into a saucepan with remaining sugar mixture. Return to heat and cook for two minutes. Stir in vanilla. Arrange in a deep casserole dish and alternate layers of vanilla wafers, banana slices and pudding. Top the mixture with pudding. Beat egg whites until soft peaks form. Gradually add remaining sugar (1/3 cup) and beat until it forms a stiff meringue. Spread meringue over pudding. Bake in oven set at 350 degrees for 15 minutes.

Bread Pudding

Yields: 6-8 servings

3 cups French bread, cubed (or day old bread)
2 tbls. butter or margarine
6 tbls. sugar
1 tsp. vanilla
4 tbls. sugar

1/4 cup raisins
2 eggs, separated
1-1/4 cups milk
1/4 tsp. cream of tartar
1/4-1/2 cup of water

Directions:

Moisten bread cubes with water. Squeeze to remove excess water. Stir in raisins and softened butter. Pour into a greased one quart casserole dish. Beat egg yolks and 6 tablespoons of sugar. Add milk and vanilla. Pour over bread mixture. Bake in 350 degree oven for 45 minutes.

Meringue Topping (optional)
Beat egg whites and cream of tartar until soft peaks form. While continuing to beat, gradually add 4 tablespoons sugar. Spoon meringue over pudding and return to oven for 15 minutes.

Mama's Round Steak Madrid

2 round steaks
1/2 lb. bacon
1 medium onion, chopped
1 medium bell pepper, chopped
1/2 tsp. minced garlic
2 tbls. chopped celery
1 tbls. green chiles
1 can (8 oz.) tomatoes
1 can (8 oz.) tomato sauce
1 can (8 oz.) tomato paste
2 beef bouillon cubes
1/2 tsp. chile powder

flour (for dusting)
salt
pepper
1/2 stick butter
1/4 tsp. oregano
1 tbls. Worcestershire sauce
1 tbls. Tabasco sauce
1/4 tsp. thyme
1/4 cup sherry
1 cup shredded cheddar cheese
1/3 cup pimentos (optional)

Directions:
Preheat oven to 375 degrees. Trim rind and remove bones from the two round steaks. Dust steaks in flour, salt and pepper. Brown steaks in a skillet on both sides. Fry 1/2 lb. of bacon. Use the bacon drippings to saute the onions, bell peppers, garlic, celery and green chiles. Add tomatoes, tomato sauce and tomato paste.

Heat beef bouillon cubes, butter, and flour in a pot to make a beef gravy. Add the beef gravy to the tomato sauce over a medium heat. Add black pepper, oregano, garlic, Worcestershire sauce, Tabasco, thyme, chili powder and sherry to the sauce. Place one of the round steaks in the bottom of a casserole dish. Place sauce on the steak. Sprinkle with cheddar cheese and pimento on top of the sauce. Place the second round steak on top of the cheese. Cover the dish with aluminum foil, place in the oven and bake at 375 degrees for 45 minutes to one hour. Remove foil and if needed let steaks brown for 5-10 minutes. Serve with buttered noodles and tossed salad.

Epilogue

Grandma's hands are special. Her heart is in her hands. More important, care for your heart is in her hands. Grandma's hands are prayerful, applaud your successes, wipe away your tears, and always love unconditionally and support continually.

Well now, I hope that this journey into the culture of my family's traditions has evoked some warm memories of your past. Memories that I hope you will record with as much joy and pleasure as I have. I'll be the first to admit that some recipes are very intense. But, try a few, add your personal touch and let me know how they turn out.

As I mentioned initially, I never thought my family was totally normal. However, it wasn't until much later in this process that I learned how truly unique we are. Chronicling my families' culture has truly been a labor of love. I trust that you will feel and share a little bit of this love as you move along life's journey.

Now to prove just how truly creative we really are, I'll sign off with our family song (our version of "Side by Side," written in 1927 by Harry Woods). We sang this song after our annual family Christmas show.

Side by Side

(written by Harry Woods, 1927)

"Oh we ain't gotta a barrel of money,
and maybe we're ragged and funny
but, we'll travel along singin' a song side by side.

We don't know what's comin' tomorrow,
maybe it's trouble and sorrow
but, we'll travel the road singin' our song,
side by side.

Thru all kinds of weather,
what if the skies should fall,
Just as long as we're together
It really doesn't matter at all.

When they've all had their quarrels and parted,
We'll be the same as we started
just travelin' along singin' our song
side by side."

Appendix - Measurements, Substitutions and Definitions

Equivalents

Liquid Measure Volume Equivalents
3 teaspoons = 1 tablespoon
2 tablespoons = 1 fluid ounce
4 tablespoons = 1/4 cup
5 tablespoons + 1 teaspoon = 1/3 cup
8 tablespoons = 1/2 cup or 4 ounces
16 tablespoons = 1 cup or 8 ounces
3/8 cup = 1/4 cup plus 2 tablespoons
5/8 cup = ½ cup plus 2 tablespoons
7/8 cup = 3/4 cup plus 2 tablespoons
1 cup = ½ pint or 8 ounces
2 cups = 1 pint or 16 ounces
1 quart = 2 pints or 64 tablespoons
1 gallon = 4 quarts

Dry Measure Volume Equivalents
2 cups = 1 pint
2 pints = 1 quart
4 quarts = 1 gallon

Butter or Margarine Measurements
1 pound = 4 sticks or 2 cups
1 cup = 2 sticks
½ cup = 1 stick
1/4 cup = ½ stick

Miscellaneous Measure Equivalents
Pinch = As much as can be taken between tip of finger and thumb
6 dashes = 1 teaspoon
8 teaspoons = 1 ounce

Yields and Equivalents

Eggs (large)
> whites, 1 cup = 8 to 10
> whole, 1 cup = 4 to 6
> yolks, 1 cup = 12 to 14

Flour (all-purpose)
> 4 cups = 1 pound

Garlic
> 1 clove = ½ tsp minced

Green pepper
> ½ cup chopped = 1 small
> 1 cup chopped = 1 medium

Lemon
> juice, 2 to 3 tablespoons = 1 medium lemon
> peel, 1 ½ to 3 teaspoons grated = 1 medium lemon

Onions
>green, 1 cup sliced = 9 with tops
>1 tablespoon chopped = 1 medium
>white, ½ cup chopped = 1 medium

Potatoes
>1 cup (½-inch pieces) = 1 medium
>1 cup (1/4-inch pieces) = 1 medium
>1 cup grated = 1 medium

Rice
>converted, 3 to 4 cups cooked = 1 cup uncooked
>instant, 3 cups cooked = 1 ½ cups uncooked
>regular long grain, 3 cups cooked = 1 cup uncooked
>wild, 3 cups cooked = 1 cup uncooked

Shortening
>2 cups = 1 pound

Shrimp
>2 cups cooked = 1 ½ pounds raw (in shells)

Sugar
>brown, 2 1/4 cups (firmly packed) = 1 pound
>granulated, 2 cups = 1 pound
>powdered, 4 cups = 1 pound

Ingredient Substitutions and Equivalents

Recipe Calls For:	Substitute With:
1 teaspoon baking powder	= 1/4 teaspoon baking soda plus ½ cup buttermilk

	= 1/4 teaspoon baking soda plus ½ teaspoon cream of tartar
Yeast (per cup flour)	= Use 1 1/4 teaspoon baking powder, or 1/4 teaspoon soda with 2 tablespoons vinegar
1 cup sifted all purpose flour	= 1 cup plus 2 tablespoons sifted cake flour
1 cup sifted cake flour	= 7/8 cup sifted all purpose flour
1 teaspoon sugar	= 1/4 grain saccharin = 1/8 teaspoon non-caloric sweetener
1-¾ cups packed confectioners sugar	= 1 cup granulated sugar
1 cup packed brown sugar	= 1 cup granulated sugar
1 cup butter	= 1 cup margarine = 14 tablespoons hydrogenated fat and ½ teaspoon salt = 14 tablespoons lard and ½ teaspoon salt
1 cup fresh milk	= ½ evaporated milk plus ½ cup water = ½ cup condensed milk plus ½ cup water = 4 teaspoons powdered whole milk plus 1 cup water = 4 tablespoons powdered skim milk plus 2 teaspoons butter plus 1 cup water
1 cup buttermilk or sour milk	= 1 tablespoon vinegar or lemon juice plus enough sweet milk to make one cup (let

stand 5 minutes) or 1 3/4 teaspoon
cream of tartar plus 1 cup sweet milk

1 cup buttermilk	= 1 cup yogurt
1 cup light cream	= 3 tablespoons butter and 3/4 cup milk
1 cup heavy cream	= ½ cup butter and about 3/4 cup milk

Cooking Terms

Baste - spoon a liquid over food during cooking to keep it moist.

Blanch - plunge food briefly into boiling water to preserve color, texture and nutritional value or to remove skins from fruits or nuts.

Caramelize - to melt sugar slowly over low heat until it becomes brown in color.

Coat - to cover food evenly with crumbs or a sauce.

Cube - cut into three-dimensional squares ½ inch or larger with knife.

Cut In - distribute solid fat in dry ingredients by cutting with pastry blender with a rolling motion or cutting with two knives until particles are desired size.

Dice - cut into cubes smaller than ½ inch.

Dredge - place food into flour to lightly coat.

Finely Chopped - cut into very tiny pieces.

Fold - combine ingredients lightly using two motions. First, cut vertically through mixture with rubber spatula. Next, slide spatula across bottom of bowl and up the side, turning the mixture over. Continue down-across-up-over motion while rotating bowl 1/4 turn with each series of strokes.

Garnish - to decorate the food served with additional foods that have distinctive color or texture, such as parsley, fresh berries or carrot curls.

Glaze - to brush or drizzle a mixture on a food to give it a glossy appearance, hard finish or decoration.

Marinate - let food stand in a savory (usually acidic) liquid for several hours to add flavor or to tenderize.

Panfry - beginning with a cold skillet, to fry in little or no fat.

Parboil - partially or pre-boil food until tender.

Poach - cook in hot liquid kept just below the boiling point.

Reduce - boil liquid uncovered to evaporate liquid and intensify flavor.

Saute - foods cooked in hot oil or margarine over medium-high heat with frequent tossing and turning motion.

Score - cut surface of food about 1/4 inch deep with knife to facilitate cooking, flavoring or tenderizing.

Soft Peaks - egg whites beaten until peaks stand up straight when beaters are lifted from bowl, but are still moist and glossy.

Index

114 Appendix

About the Author

Deirdre Guion is a native of Durham, North Carolina. She spent every summer and Christmas of her childhood years in New Orleans, Louisiana, with her mother's family. Deirdre comes from a long line of cooks including a grandmother who managed a parochial school cafeteria for 15 years to "Chef Bob" her uncle who has been featured on the Great Chef's of New Orleans series. Deirdre started cooking around age nine with guidance from her grandmother, mother and uncle. She still enjoys cooking for family and friends.

Deirdre received her undergraduate degree in Economics from Spelman College in 1986 and her Masters of Business Administration from the Fuqua School of Business, Duke University. Her work experience includes banking at Wachovia Bank in Corporate Loan Administration and Marketing at General Mills in Minneapolis, Minnesota. Currently Deirdre is co-owner and Vice President of Niche Communications Inc., a full service marketing and advertising agency in North Carolina. Deirdre works with clients such as Maybelline and Hanes Hosiery.

In 1995, she traveled extensively with Civil Rights matriarch, Rosa Parks in connection the 40th anniversary of the Sit In Movement. She is an Adjunct Instructor in the Department of Business and Economics at Winston-Salem State University. Deirdre is an active member of the Winston-Salem Alumnae Chapter of Delta Sigma Theta Sorority, Inc.

Deirdre's vision is to motivate the reader to celebrate their family ties, relationships and cultural heritage with good food and good company.

CAP'S PUBLICATIONS

From the Garden of Eden to America by Avaneda D. Hobbs, Ed.D.
        The function of this book is to provide an in-depth study of the black man, the black church, black leadership, and the social implications of these ingredients within mainstream America. Here is the biblical history of the black man, a prognosis of the black church, and insight into the social and psychological position of the black man about his religion. The book discusses the biblical beginnings of the black man's slavery, the scriptural significance of the Garden of Eden and the history of the races, the origin of the American black church, and a detailed description of all black religious bodies in the United States. Original photos of the denomination's leaders, from the 1700s to the 1900s, are included. Further, this book examines the ingredients required for training effective black leaders in building churches and their role in building an influential church, from an evangelistic point of view. It also provides a comprehensive model to track black churches in any given geographical area in the U.S.

Who Are We? Building A Knowledge Base About Different Ethnic, Racial, and Cultural Groups in America by Avaneda D. Hobbs, Ed.D.
        Experts in diversity agree that the question is whether one's knowledge base can adequately prepare them to lead and gain a competitive edge at their place of influence. This book was prepared to help in presenting one-hour workshops on diversity or cultural awareness. The main goal is to increase one's knowledge base to function in a diverse workforce. It contains self-paced study modules on the different ethnic, racial and cultural groups in America. Each presents the historical background, belief systems and current profiles on the different groups. It provides a step-by-step guide on how to conduct diversity workshops.

What Pest Control Companies Don't Want You to Know by Roosevelt McNeil, Jr.
        Here is an in-depth study of the pest control industry. It elaborates on how some pest control companies rip you off and what they don't tell you that can not only be hazardous to your health, but also to your wallet. This book is designed to provide information to consumers on how to eliminate pests from their home on a permanent basis, how to identify potential problems as a result of unwanted pests, and how to use simple solutions to ward off future problems. Learn the quickest way of killing termites, the best insecticides to get from your local stores, and the best ways of getting rid of mosquitoes. Includes extensive graphics that describe the most common pests and information on providing a pest free environment, as well as a list of reputable pest control companies.

The New Age Millennium: An Exposé of Symbols, Slogans and Hidden Agendas by Demond Wilson (formerly of Sanford and Son)
        This book is a remarkable integration of traditional and contemporary wisdom borne out of the authors' 14 years' rich experience in the worldwide religious arena. The New Age Millennium: An Exposé of Symbols, Slogans and Hidden Agendas is one of the most illuminating books on the New Age movement, one world government, humanism, religion, the Illuminati and Free Masonry. Discover the answers to perplexing questions about where this world is headed to.

ORDER FORM

Type your name, shipping address and telephone number:

Name _____

Company Name _____

Shipping Address _____

City _____

State/Province _____ ZIP/Postal Code _____

Daytime Phone (_____) _____
(In case we have a question about your order)

Please check your product choice here:

DESCRIPTION	QUANTITY	PRICE	TOTAL

Calculate your total cost and indicate method of payment:

Product Cost	$	
US Sales Tax	$	
Freight	$3.00	
Total Cost	$	

Payment method: (Make checks payable to CAP Publishing & Literary Co.)

Check/money order

Mastercard

VISA

Credit Card No.

Expiration Date

Cardholder's Signature

CAP PUBLISHING & LITERARY CO.
P.O. Box 531403
Forestville, MD 20753
CAP's e-mail: drvickihay@pobox.com